IDEAS FOR
ACTIVE LEARNING
GRADES K-2

Literature-Based
Workshops
for Mathematics

HIGH/SCOPE ELEMENTARY CURRICULUM MATERIALS

Ideas for Active Learning, Grades K–2 Series
Literature-Based Workshops for Language Arts

Elementary Curriculum Guides
Foundations in Elementary Education: Movement
Foundations in Elementary Education: Music
Foundations in Elementary Education: Overview
Language & Literacy
Learning Environment
Mathematics
Science

Elementary Science Activity Series
Life and Environment
Structure and Form
Energy and Change

Elementary Curriculum Videotapes
Active Learning
Classroom Environment
Language & Literacy
Mathematics

Related Movement and Music Materials
*Teaching Movement & Dance: A Sequential Approach to
   Rhythmic Movement,* 4th Edition
*Movement Plus Music: Activities for
   Children Ages 3 to 7,* 2nd Edition
Movement Plus Rhymes, Songs, & Singing Games
Movement in Steady Beat
Rhythmically Moving 1–9 (cassette, CD)
Guides to Rhythmically Moving 1–4
Changing Directions 1–6 (cassette, CD)
*Foundations in Elementary Education:
   Music Recordings* (cassette, CD)
Rhythmically Walking (cassette)

Program Evaluation
Elementary Program Implementation Profile (PIP)

Available from
High/Scope® Press
A division of the
High/Scope Educational Research Foundation
600 North River Street, Ypsilanti, MI 48198-2898

ORDERS: phone (800)40-PRESS, fax (800)442-4FAX
e-mail: *press@highscope.org*
Web site: *www.highscope.org*

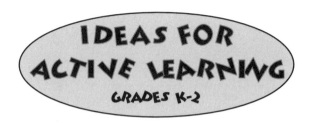

IDEAS FOR
ACTIVE LEARNING
GRADES K-2

Literature-Based Workshops

for Mathematics

Kathy Morrison, Tina Dittrich, & Jill Claridge

HIGH/SCOPE® PRESS

Ypsilanti, Michigan

Published by

High/Scope® Press

A division of the High/Scope Educational Research Foundation
600 North River Street
Ypsilanti, Michigan 48198-2898
(734)485-2000, fax (734)485-0704
press@highscope.org

Editor: Holly Barton
Cover design, text design, and production: Judy Seling, Seling Design
Illustrations: Kyle Raetz

Library of Congress Cataloging-in-Publication Data

Morrison, Kathy.
   Literature-based workshops for mathematics : ideas for active learning, grades K-2 /
Kathy Morrison, Tina Dittrich & Jill Claridge.
       p. cm.
Includes bibliographical references and index.
  ISBN 1-57379-167-9 (pbk. : alk. paper)
 1. Mathematics--Study and teaching (Primary) 2. Children's literature in mathematics
education. I. Dittrich, Tina, 1969- II. Claridge, Jill,
1949- III. Title.
 QA135.6 .M69 2002
 372.7'044--dc21

                        2002002890

Printed in the United States of America
10 9 8 7 6 5 4 3 2 1

CONTENTS

HOW BIG? HOW WIDE? HOW TALL? 155

STUDENT INSTRUCTION CARDS 187

INDEX 205

ACKNOWLEDGMENTS

We greatly appreciate the contributions of the following teachers, who field-tested the workshops in this book; gave us feedback on them; and contributed photographs, samples of their students' work, and ideas for handouts. Many thanks go to Chris Vogelsberg, Mary Aldridge, Jackie Shock, and Lila Mitchell, Bessie Hoffman Elementary, Belleville, MI; Elizabeth Pick, Loretta Lee, and Betsy Keisling, Livingston Developmental Academy, Howell, MI; Kathleen Peterson and Alice Reidl, To'Hajiilee-He School, Cañoncito, NM; Nicole Doda, Hillcrest School, Florence, WI; Jennifer Fichtner, St. Marks School, Sierra Madre, CA; and Kiki Boteler, Kickapoo Nation School, Powhattan, KS. We also thank Diana Jo Johnston for coordinating this field testing.

We also acknowledge the publications staff at High/Scope Educational Research Foundation for bringing this book to fruition: Lynn Taylor, Holly Barton, and Pattie McDonald.

IDEAS FOR
ACTIVE LEARNING
GRADES K-2

Literature-Based Workshops

for Mathematics

INTRODUCTION

This book is designed to provide ideas for planning math workshop experiences that are rich in content and exciting for students in kindergarten through grade 2. These workshops draw on a wealth of children's literature revolving around such topics as counting, shapes, sequencing, addition, money, and measurement. Many of the books used in the workshops are children's classics that teachers are already reading with their students simply for enjoyment. The workshop plans presented here enable students to go one step further and thoroughly explore a book and the concepts or experiences it presents. We hope to show teachers the invaluable resource good children's literature can be for enhancing a content area. This collection of workshops emphasizes math concepts, but skills and concepts from other content areas have also been integrated into many of the activities.

Each section of this book contains nine workshops built around a selection of children's books that are similar in theme or genre. The workshops are not intended to be complete, sequenced math units. Instead, the workshop instructions are offered as a starting point to help teachers develop their own ideas and plans. Teachers who are using the workshops in this book will probably want to use them along with many additional instructional activities, including computer activities.

Workshops may begin with the teacher's reading a story that goes along with the activity, as shown here. In other workshops, children may read or review the story themselves, or listen to a recording of it.

We encourage you to choose the workshops from this book that best suit your teaching style and the needs and interests of your group of children. Feel free to adapt and refine them for your students. We strongly urge you to seek out the excellent works of children's literature that accompany each activity (see p. 210 for information on locating or ordering these books). If you are not able to obtain the book needed for a workshop, in some cases you may substitute other high-quality storybooks for those listed. Check the resource list at the end of each section of this book for recommendations for alternatives. A good children's librarian can also be helpful in choosing additional books.

As you plan workshops around the ideas presented in this book, we encourage you to follow the workshop guidelines given in High/Scope training and in the High/Scope resources listed on p. 11. The following description of High/Scope workshops is adapted from these materials.

WHAT IS A HIGH/SCOPE WORKSHOP?

The workshops in this book were designed for programs using the High/Scope elementary approach. However, the activities may be used in any elementary program that emphasizes active, hands-on learning and independent small-group work. In High/Scope programs, workshops are the instructional periods of the day—the times when students focus on specific concepts and skills in basic content areas, such as math, language arts, or science. A workshop period may focus on a single content area, such as math, or on a combination of subjects.

Workshop periods take place two or more times a day and last an hour or more. A typical day's schedule, for example, might include three 1-hour workshop periods, one for language arts, one for math, and one for social studies alternating with science. During any workshop period, there will be four to six different small groups meeting at the same time, with three to six children in each group. In a class of 20 students, for example, the teacher might plan for four workshop groups of five children each; in a class of 27, there might be six groups with four or five children each.

Within each group, students may work cooperatively or individually, depending on the assigned task. Workshops are intended as an alternative to traditional worksheets and seatwork. As such, they are designed to encourage students to make choices, solve problems, and learn by doing. Even though High/Scope teachers assign specific tasks for each workshop, they plan the experience so that it offers students some element of choice.

During workshop activities, students have many opportunities for communicating and problem-solving with one another.

A workshop period or a series of workshop periods may be organized in many different ways, depending upon the preferences and experience of the teacher. A simple arrangement, often chosen by teachers who are just beginning to use small-group instruction, is to have all of the small groups work on the same task (workshop) at the same time. Another simple way of organizing workshops is to have two different workshop experiences going simultaneously, with half the small groups working on each one. In the middle of the workshop period, the two sets of groups trade materials. Another arrangement, one preferred by many experienced High/Scope teachers, is to plan a workshop rotation consisting of four to six groups, each doing a different workshop. The small groups rotate

through the workshops until each group has completed all of them. (This may take more than one workshop period, spread out over several days.)

To prepare for a workshop rotation, the teacher sets out the materials for the workshop at separate tables or areas. When children change workshops, they change places as well. Therefore it is important for each small group, before rotating, to clean up their table or area and reorganize the materials for the next group. For example, to prepare for a second-grade math workshop period on money with six rotating groups, the teacher might set materials out for the following experiences:

- Group 1: Students find as many combinations of coins as possible that equal $1.00, an activity from section 5 of this book.

- Group 2: Students figure the cost of milk for the whole class, another activity from section 5.

- Group 3: Students work on problems from the math text.

- Group 4: Students work on a math-related computer activity.

- Group 5: Students make a graph showing the number of each type of coin in a jar.

- Group 6: Students play a commercial or teacher-made money or other math-related game.

In a workshop rotation that includes four to six groups, the students work on one workshop for a designated time, usually 10 to 30 minutes. Then the teacher gives a signal, and the first group moves from the first workshop to the second, the second group moves from the second workshop to the third, and so on. (The last group would rotate to the first workshop). This continues until all the groups have cycled through all the workshops, or a set number of them, in which case students would rotate through the rest the following day.

The time students spend at each task in a rotation cycle and the length of time needed to complete the entire set of workshops will vary depending on the age of the students, their experience with the workshop process, and the nature of the tasks assigned. If you were designing a math rotation of six workshops, for example, you would need to decide how many workshop periods you would need for the children to complete the cycle. For example, the class might do three workshops one day and three the next, or do two each day for three days. Typically, kindergartners and first-graders (as well as children new to the rotation process), spend 10 or 15 minutes on each workshop, and students may cycle through four or five workshops during one math workshop period. Older, more experienced children who can handle more extended activities may

work for 20 to 30 minutes on each of two or three workshops, completing the rest of the workshops during the following day's math workshop time or during workshop periods on the next two days.

With four to six activities going on simultaneously, students must be able to work without direct adult supervision for much of the workshop period. We have designed most of the workshops in this book so that children can carry them out independently, working with the support of the other members of their group. Some of the activities are designated as teacher-facilitated; these require the adult to work directly with the children during all or part of the workshop.

During the workshop period, teachers may devote the majority of their attention to one of the small groups for more intensive instruction. However, whenever possible, teachers divide their attention among all the workshops, giving guidance and assistance when needed as children work semi-independently with their group. Some workshops may be more effective when the teacher facilitates or models the activities the first day and students complete them independently the next day.

ADVANTAGES OF THE WORKSHOP APPROACH

The workshop format for instruction has many advantages for both teachers and students. Working in small groups means students can work according to their individual abilities and interests. Workshops provide experiences in working independently that promote children's self-reliance and enable them to develop problem-solving skills. Workshops also create opportunities for cooperative work and communication with classmates that are not available to children during traditional whole-group teaching. In addition, because most children are working on their own for much of the workshop period, the teacher is able to give individual attention to students when needed or to work with a few students on

a focused task. Also, because each workshop involves only a few children at a time, they give children a chance to work directly with shared resources and equipment—such as science instruments, computers, or reference books—that would be too costly to provide for every student.

Workshop projects enable students to practice and apply important basic skills in meaningful settings.

Another important aspect of small-group workshops is that they are engaging and fun for children. As a result, they motivate children to master important skills and concepts. They offer opportunities for children to work on realistic projects that are meaningful to them; to relate academic tasks to their own interests, ideas, and goals; and to learn through hands-on experiences. These active learning experiences are usually far more relevant and involving for children than, for example, filling out a worksheet or listening to a teacher lecture. While a typical small-group workshop may not expose children to as many concepts and skills as the teacher could present in a whole-group lesson lasting a comparable time, children's more active involvement in small-group experiences results in learning that is more likely to stay with them.

Writing tasks are more meaningful when they are expressions of what children know and have discovered, such as through their explorations with materials.

This book assumes that teachers have taken some time to prepare their students for workshops and that students are comfortable with the process and organization of workshops. If you are now teaching in a traditional setting emphasizing whole-class experiences and you want to use small groups for more of your instruction, bear in mind that making this shift in approach is a long-term process. If you need tips for getting started with workshop-based instruction, we suggest you read "Suggestions for Helping Students Work Independently" (see pp. 9–11), consult other High/Scope curriculum materials, and attend High/Scope training to gain a better understanding of the workshop process.

HOW THIS BOOK IS ORGANIZED

This book is made up of the following six sections: "I Spy a Shape" (kindergarten); "1, 2, 3, A Counting Spree!" (kindergarten); "Big, Small, and In Between: Ordering, Comparing, and Measuring" (first grade); *"12 Ways to Get to 11:* A Study in Addition" (first grade); "Ten Pennies for a Dime" (second grade); and "How Big? How Wide? How Tall?" (second grade). Although each set of workshops has a suggested grade level, the workshops can be adapted to fit other age groups.

Each section begins with a chart, titled **Workshops at a Glance,** that briefly summarizes the workshops in that section. Following this is an overview of the books used in the section and the skills and concepts emphasized.

Each section also includes a teacher-led **Whole-Group Introductory Lesson,** designed to prepare the class for the set of workshops that follow. In this lesson, the class as a group reads or listens to one or more of the children's books that go along with that set of workshops. Then the whole group carries out a few activities that relate to those they will be doing independently in their workshop groups.

In the pages that follow each whole-group lesson, complete instructions are given for the individual workshops in that section. The following components are included for each workshop:

- **Story.** The title of the book, song, or computer program that goes with the workshop. Since each book is described in the introductory section, just the title is given here (and the author when the book is first mentioned).

- **Workshop summary.** A brief summary of the activity.

- **Key experiences.** A list of several High/Scope elementary key experiences that students are likely to engage in during this workshop. (The key experiences are statements of important concepts and processes in various areas of learning.) Note that since all workshop activities are somewhat open-ended, additional learning experiences not listed here may also occur, depending upon the direction students take.

- **Materials.** A list of materials needed for the workshop.

- **Instructions.** Step-by-step directions for the workshop. Some workshops include a mini-lesson at the beginning. This is a brief teacher-facilitated introduction to skills or concepts students will need to carry out the rest of the activity independently.

- **Assessment.** Suggestions for activities to evaluate the outcomes of the workshop. These may include evaluations of students' work, teacher observations, or student self-assessments.

- **Extensions.** Ideas for follow-up activities.

- **Modifications.** Suggestions for simplifying the activity or for modifying it for students with special needs, or simply alternative ways to do the workshop.

- **Student instructions.** Simple, illustrated directions for the workshop, written for students to read and follow independently. These are located near the back of the book. See suggestions in the next section for using the student instructions effectively. (Student instructions are included only for student-initiated workshops.)

- **Workshop handouts.** Ready-to-duplicate materials needed to complete the workshop successfully (not all workshops utilize handouts). These are located after the workshop they accompany.

SUGGESTIONS FOR HELPING STUDENTS WORK INDEPENDENTLY

We've tried to make our instructions as complete as possible, but it will still take careful planning, as well as experience with the workshop process, to make your workshops run smoothly. Here are some tips for more effective workshops:

• **Think carefully about your workshop groupings.** Attempt to balance each group by such factors as ability, gender, personality, and tendency to be a leader or a follower. Separate children whose personalities may conflict. Change the groupings at regular intervals so that children have a chance to work with a variety of other children.

Workshops provide a positive social environment that supports children's intrinsic motivation to learn.

• **When introducing workshops for the first time, focus on the workshop *process* first, then introduce subject area content.** Set up a few nonthreatening, short, fun activities for the children, such as simple games or story tapes. Have children rotate through four or five such workshops in one workshop period, changing every 10–15 minutes. Be sure to include time for students to clean up the materials and prepare the game or activity for the next group. Do this several times. Once children understand how the rotation works and are comfortable with the process of working in small groups, introduce longer workshop activities with more challenging content.

• **At the beginning of a workshop period, briefly demonstrate or explain all the workshops in the rotation to the group as a whole.** A 5- to 10-minute introduction is usually sufficient to explain what students will be doing at each workshop. Sometimes, however, students will need to be introduced in advance to skills and concepts they will need for the small-group activities. In these cases, a mini-lesson is included with the workshop instructions. You can do the mini-lesson with the whole group at the start of the workshop, or plan it for a previous day if you think students need more practice with a concept. If your students already have experience with the skills and concepts involved, they may not need the mini-lesson and can move directly into the independent part of the workshop.

- **Appoint student leaders for each workshop rotation.** Whenever a new workshop rotation cycle begins, meet with the student leaders before class or during recess to acquaint them with the activities included in the rotation. The 15 minutes or so you spend planning with the leaders will save you time later on. During this time, you can prepare the student leaders to answer the group members' questions about the logistics of the workshop: what steps are included; where the materials are located; where to go if they need additional materials; whether group members will be working by themselves, with partners, or cooperatively with the rest of the group; where to put completed projects; and so forth. Another part of the student leader's role during the workshop may be to carry questions he or she can't answer to the teacher. Since many students will ask the same kinds of questions, this is another way to limit the demands on the teacher during the workshop session. Rotate the leader's role frequently so that all students have a chance to hold this position.

- **Encourage students to use the student instructions provided with the activity.** You can provide multiple copies of the instructions, write them on the chalkboard, or tape-record them for nonreaders. Kindergarten children may not be able to use the instructions independently; however, kindergarten classrooms often have aides or parent volunteers who will find it helpful to refer to the student instructions as they work with the children.

- **During workshops, encourage children to work independently by having children with questions or problems turn to peers first, then to you if necessary.** For example, some teachers have an "Ask three children before me" rule. You might also have a sign-up sheet for students who haven't been able to solve a problem by working with a classmate. You can respond to these requests for help at the first available moment, working down the list of those with questions.

Students learn to use one another as resources as they complete workshop activities together.

- **If a workshop in this book is designated as teacher-facilitated, think carefully about how you can give the students in this workshop group the extra help they will need.** Keep in mind that you may not need to remain with this group for the entire workshop period. You may need to be there just for part of the activity, then remain nearby to give them additional help with problems that arise. Because of the extra supervision needed for the teacher-facilitated workshops, don't include more than one during any given workshop period.

- **If parents or older students are available, ask them to help at workshop times.** Again, the volunteers can refer to the student instructions as they assist children with the workshops.

For successful workshops, use the suggestions above with patience and persistence. While the workshop approach to instruction may take more effort at first, you'll find that your quality time with students will increase gradually as students take on more responsibility for their own learning.

CONCLUSION

The workshops in this book are designed as a starting point for your own ideas. As you gain experience doing High/Scope-style workshops, you will probably want to begin designing your own, referring to this book as a source of ideas. As you grow accustomed to the workshop process and learn to develop teaching ideas from children's literature, you will be amazed at the rich and exciting active learning experiences you can provide for your students.

HIGH/SCOPE RESOURCES ON THE WORKSHOP PROCESS

Albro, Cathy, Johnston, Diana Jo, and Brickman, Nancy. (1998). Elementary learning: Encouraging young problem solvers. High/Scope *Extensions* (September): 5.

Brickman, Nancy. (2000). Workshops—*not* one size fits all! High/Scope *Extensions* (September): 5.

Hohmann, Charles. (1994). K–3 Learning: Elementary-level small groups. High/Scope *Extensions* (March/April): 5.

I SPY
A SHAPE

KINDERGARTEN

I SPY A SHAPE
Workshops at a Glance

Food Collage Students create a collage of food pictures from magazines or food advertisements. *The Very Hungry Caterpillar.*	**Shape Twisting*** Students play an "entangling" movement-based game with shapes.	**Toothpick Triangles*** Students experiment with toothpicks to discover how shapes can be changed by adding, taking away, or moving sides. *The Greedy Triangle.*
Shape Sculpture Students make shapes out of pipe cleaners, then combine the shapes to create a 3-d sculpture. *The Greedy Triangle.*	**Shape Hunt** Students go on a shape hunt in the classroom and draw objects that are different shapes. *Shapes, Shapes, Shapes.*	**Pattern Block Pictures** Students create a design with pattern blocks, then use die-cut paper shapes to reproduce the pattern on construction paper. *Shapes, Shapes, Shapes.*
I Spy Shapes Students write and illustrate a shape book. *Round Is a Mooncake: A Book About Shapes.*	**Computer Shapes*** Students create pictures with shapes on a computer program, then write or dictate a sentence about their pictures. *Millie's Math House.*	**Singing About Shapes*** Students learn a shape song and act out the movements.

*Requires direct teacher involvement during all or part of the workshop

This set of workshops centers on shapes. The activities take students beyond identifying basic shapes to examining what makes them different from one another—for example, edges, corners, and curves—and combining them into more complex shapes. Students will make shape sculptures, write and illustrate a shape book, and go on a hunt for shapes in the environment. Other workshops use shapes to get children up and moving in a variety of ways.

Four books accompany these shape workshops, although there are many other books on this topic that you could use as well. As many kindergarten students are likely to be familiar with basic shapes, look for books that, like the ones suggested here, deal with shapes in a more complex way or encourage children to look at shapes from a slightly different angle.

The Very Hungry Caterpillar by Eric Carle introduces children to the shape study. The ravenous caterpillar eats foods of several different shapes, including triangular pie and rectangular cheese.

The triangle in Marilyn Burns's *The Greedy Triangle* is not satisfied with his shape, so he asks the shape-shifter to change him into another one. After several such changes, each time gaining one more side and another angle, he realizes that being himself is best after all!

Tana Hoban's books are well known for their unique photographs picturing common objects in uncommon ways. In her book *Shapes, Shapes, Shapes,* children will discover shapes in their environment that perhaps they never noticed before.

Another shapes-in-the-environment book is *Round Is a Mooncake: A Book About Shapes* by Roseanne Thong. As an Asian American girl explores her home and neighborhood, she notices shapes in both universally recognized objects and some of cultural origin—such as round rice bowls and rectangular Chinese lace.

There are four teacher-facilitated workshops in this section, along with a whole-group introductory lesson.

I SPY A SHAPE
Whole-Group Introductory Lesson

MATERIALS

- *The Very Hungry Caterpillar* by Eric Carle
- Chalkboard or large sheet of newsprint and marker

INSTRUCTIONS

Ask children to name all the shapes they can think of. Draw these shapes on the board and write the names next to them. Discuss the characteristics of each shape, including corners, faces, curves, and edges. Have the class compare the shapes based on these characteristics.

Read *The Very Hungry Caterpillar* to the class. In this story the caterpillar is busily enjoying a variety of foods in various shapes. Ask the children to name the foods in the story that are shaped like a circle, square, rectangle, triangle, and any other shapes. Then ask the children to name additional foods they can think of that match each shape. On newsprint or the chalkboard, write the name of the shapes and the corresponding foods as children suggest them. It may be difficult to come up with foods for some shapes, such as a heart, but children will enjoy the challenge and may even surprise you! (Many foods can be cut into a heart shape, such as cookies, gelatin, and bread.)

After you finish discussing the shapes in the story, introduce each of the workshops to the whole group so children have an idea of what they will be doing later on.

FOOD COLLAGE

STORY

The Very Hungry Caterpillar by Eric Carle

WORKSHOP SUMMARY

Students create a collage of food pictures from magazines or food advertisements. This activity is student-directed; children complete the activity by following the student instructions.

INSTRUCTIONS

1. Each child chooses a die-cut shape. If there are more children in the group than there are different shapes, more than one child can choose the same shape.

2. The children glue their shape at the top of their construction paper.

3. Children look through the magazines and advertisements and cut out pictures of foods that are the same shape as the one on their paper.

4. Children glue the pictures onto the construction paper.

ASSESSMENT

• Note whether children accurately match foods with their shapes.

• Take anecdotal notes as children work, noting in particular the language they use and how they decide which shape a more complex food belongs under (for instance, a piece of chicken).

EXTENSIONS

• Encourage children to be caterpillars looking for food in the magazines and ads.

KEY EXPERIENCES

Speaking & listening (Language & literacy)—
• Using language to solve problems

Collections of objects (Math)—
• Sorting a collection, then re-sorting with new criteria

Geometry & space (Math)—
• Identifying attributes of 2-d objects (corners, faces, curves, and edges); sorting by shape
• Constructing with 2-d, 3-d shapes; recognizing like shapes, naming simple shapes (circle, square, triangle, cube, cone)

MATERIALS

• Die-cut shapes (circle, square, triangle, rectangle, cone). If die-cuts are not available, make your own.
• Construction paper (one sheet per child)
• Assorted magazines and food advertisements that contain pictures of foods
• Scissors
• Glue

- Have children bring in foods from home that are of various shapes or explore their lunch bags for food shapes. Or, bring in a variety of "shape foods" for children to explore and sort. Are there foods that don't seem to fit any particular shape?

- Have students count the number of foods in their collages. Which shapes were easiest to find? Which were hardest?

MODIFICATIONS

- Have precut pictures of foods for children to glue onto their construction paper.

- If children have difficulty finding a particular food shape, have them cut out any type of pictures they can find in that shape.

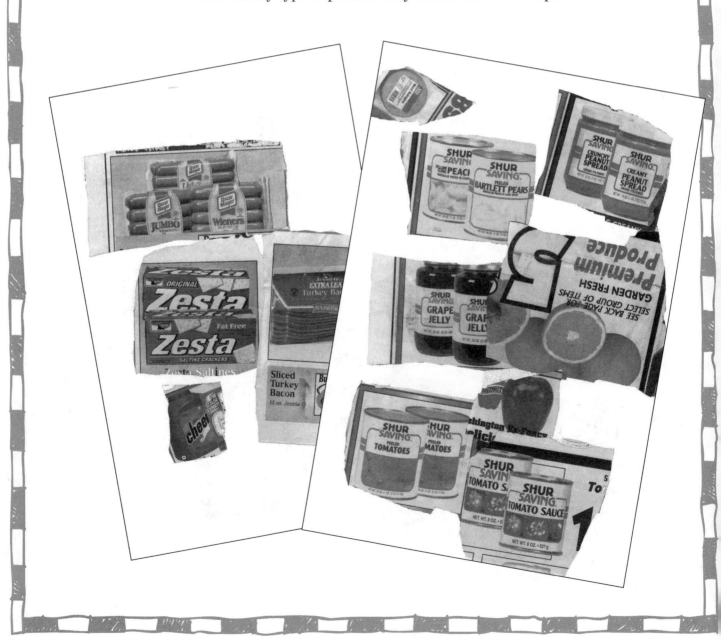

SHAPE TWISTING

WORKSHOP SUMMARY

In this teacher-facilitated workshop, students play an entangling movement-based game with shapes.

INSTRUCTIONS (TEACHER-FACILITATED)

Preparation:

Use the shower curtain to make a game board similar to the game Twister, using shapes instead of colors. Use electrical tape to make five rows of shapes across the curtain and five columns down. Make a variety of circles, squares, triangles, and rectangles. (See sample diagram at right.)

Make two spinners with four sections each. On the first spinner draw two hands and two feet; label each foot and hand with either *R* or *L* for right and left. On the second spinner draw a circle, square, triangle, and rectangle.

Workshop:

1. Children decide who begins the game.

2. The child spins the first spinner to see which body part he or she will use. The child then spins the second spinner to find out which shape to place the body part on. Assist children with identifying right and left if necessary.

3. After spinning both spinners, the child places the designated hand or foot on the indicated shape on the shower curtain (for example, right hand on a circle).

4. All children take a turn spinning and joining the others on the shower curtain. Children will probably become entangled as they place their hands and feet on the different shapes!

5. When all the children are on the mat, continue to spin for them so that they all have several body parts on the shapes. This should be enjoyable and funny! Continue to play until the end of workshop time.

KEY EXPERIENCES

Movement—
- Acting upon movement directions
- Moving in locomotor ways

Geometry & space (Math)—
- Naming simple shapes

MATERIALS

- One solid-colored shower curtain
- Electrical tape
- Two blank spinners with four sections each

ASSESSMENT

- Observe children's dexterity, body control, and knowledge of shapes.

EXTENSIONS

- Have the group design a shape game, for example, one similar to Candy Land.

- Write a group story about playing the shape twisting game. Encourage the children to use shape words and to describe how they were entangled during the game.

MODIFICATIONS

- Give children some time to practice left/right concepts and following directions using these concepts.

- To help children identify right and left, write *R* and *L* on small pieces of tape and have children stick them on their hands and feet.

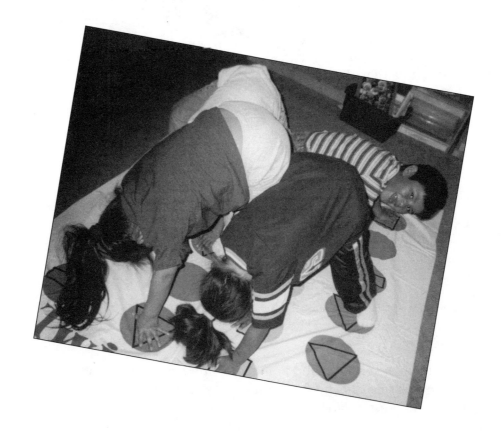

TOOTHPICK TRIANGLES

STORY

The Greedy Triangle by Marilyn Burns

WORKSHOP SUMMARY

Students experiment with toothpicks to discover how shapes can be formed. This activity is teacher-facilitated.

INSTRUCTIONS (TEACHER-FACILITATED)

1. Give each child three toothpicks and ask them to make a triangle. Then have them look at the first page of the story and pick out all the triangle shapes. Begin reading the story to the group. Stop when the triangle makes his first wish.

2. Ask children which shape they believe the triangle will become. Give each child another toothpick and ask them to make the new shape.

3. Continue reading the story up until the triangle is changed into a square. Ask students if they guessed correctly about his new shape. Let the group look at the page and find all the square shapes.

4. Continue this pattern of encouraging students to predict the new shape and then make it with their toothpicks (giving one more toothpick to each child each time). Ask the group what the triangle learned at the end of the story. Why was he called a greedy triangle?

5. Ask students to recall the names of the shapes they made.

ASSESSMENT

- Note children's discussion of shapes while they are making their predictions.

- Note children's ability to rearrange the toothpicks into new shapes.

KEY EXPERIENCES

Geometry & space (Math)—
- Constructing with 2-d shapes

Reading (Language & literacy)—
- Reading in specific content areas

MATERIALS

- *The Greedy Triangle* by Marilyn Burns
- Flat toothpicks (several for each child)

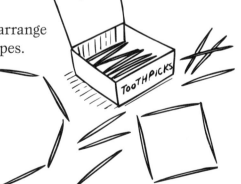

EXTENSIONS

- Take a walk around the school to find different shapes.

- Let children manipulate the toothpicks as they like.

- Have children dictate what shapes they would want to be and why. Have them illustrate their story.

MODIFICATIONS

- Have more than one book available for the group to look at.

- If children have difficulty manipulating the growing number of toothpicks, have them work in pairs.

- Read the story first, then have students work in pairs to re-create the shapes (while looking at a copy of the book).

SHAPE SCULPTURE

STORY

The Greedy Triangle

WORKSHOP SUMMARY

Students make shapes out of pipe cleaners, then combine the shapes to create a 3-d sculpture. This activity is child-directed and can be completed by following the student instructions.

INSTRUCTIONS

1. Each child makes a circle, triangle, square, and rectangle out of four different pipe cleaners. Have a representation of these shapes for children to imitate; for example, draw the shapes on the board or die-cut them and glue them to index cards.

2. Each child creates a fifth shape of his or her own choosing.

3. Students work independently, in pairs, or as a group to join their shapes together to form a sculpture. To make the shapes secure, they can twist a small pipe cleaner at the spot where the shapes join.

ASSESSMENT

- Note children's ability to create the four simple shapes and combine them to make a sculpture.

- Take Polaroid pictures of the children's creations. Using the pictures or the actual sculptures, discuss with the group the number of circles, squares, triangles, and rectangles they see in the sculpture.

EXTENSIONS

- Have children dictate a description or tell a story about their sculpture.

MODIFICATIONS

- Have children work with a partner to form the shapes.

- Hold a mini-lesson before the workshop for children to practice bending the pipe cleaners and making sharp corners.

KEY EXPERIENCES

Geometry & space (Math)—

- Constructing with 2-d and 3-d shapes
- Building complex shapes by putting simple shapes together

MATERIALS

- Pipe cleaners of various lengths

SHAPE HUNT

STORY

Shapes, Shapes, Shapes by Tana Hoban

WORKSHOP SUMMARY

Students go on a shape hunt in the classroom to find objects shaped like a circle, rectangle, square, and triangle. They then draw these objects on a chart under the column corresponding to the shape of each object. The workshop is child-directed and can be completed by following the student instructions.

INSTRUCTIONS

1. The group looks through the book, naming all the shapes on each page.

2. Each child takes a chart and a pencil and explores the room, looking for objects that fit one of the shapes on the chart.

3. Children draw a picture of these objects in the corresponding column of the chart. For example, they might draw a picture of the clock in the circle column. Children should find and draw at least one object for each shape.

ASSESSMENT

• Check charts for completion and accuracy. Do students display creativity in finding objects of various shapes?

EXTENSIONS

• Have children design a picture with a shape hidden in it.

• Have children name all the shapes seen in the room.

• Have children draw additional objects in the corresponding columns of the chart. Challenge them to find several more of each shape.

• Let children look for objects in other parts of the school or outdoors.

KEY EXPERIENCES

Observing (Science)—
• Looking at familiar things in a new way: Observing closely, systematically, and objectively

Geometry & space (Math)—
• Identifying simple shapes within complex shapes
• Naming simple shapes

MATERIALS

• *Shapes, Shapes, Shapes* by Tana Hoban
• Pencil (one per child)
• Shape chart, p. 26 (one per child)

MODIFICATIONS

- If possible, provide more than one copy of the book so children can refer to it.

- Have children work in pairs to fill in their chart.

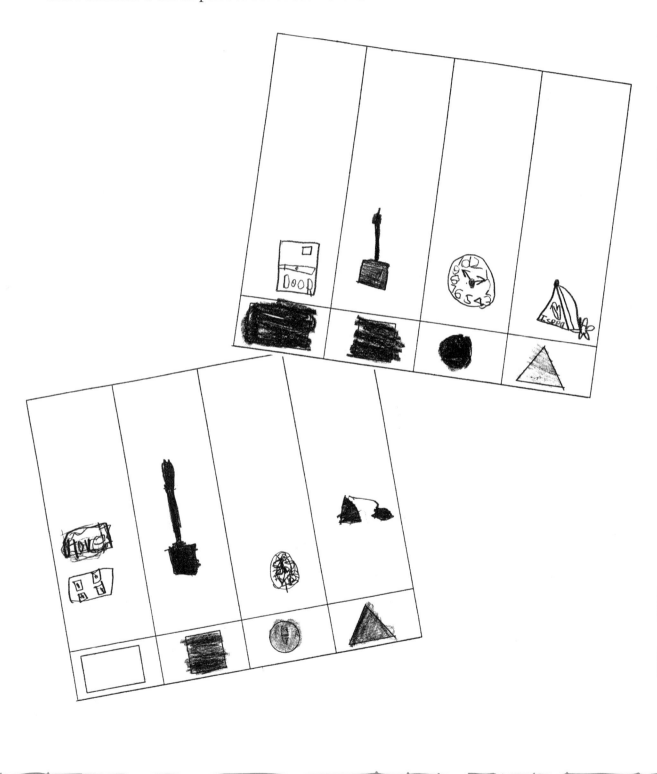

Name _____

Rectangle	Square	Circle	Triangle

[Handout 1: Shape Hunt]

PATTERN BLOCK PICTURES

STORY

Shapes, Shapes, Shapes

WORKSHOP SUMMARY

Students create a design with pattern blocks, then use die-cut paper shapes to reproduce the pattern on construction paper. This activity is child-directed and can be completed by following the student instructions.

INSTRUCTIONS

1. Each student uses the pattern blocks to make a pattern or design. All of the blocks should fit together with no spaces between.

2. Children copy their design by gluing the die-cut pattern shapes on construction paper. They begin at the top left-hand corner and proceed across the paper, then start again at the left, underneath the top row.

3. Students continue following the design, leaving no space between each paper shape.

ASSESSMENT

- Ask children what shapes they used in their design. Why, do they think, are there no circles in the pattern blocks?

- Take a Polaroid picture of children's original designs made with the pattern blocks. Compare them to the die-cut versions. Did they create and follow a pattern or design? Did they accurately reproduce the pattern with the paper shapes?

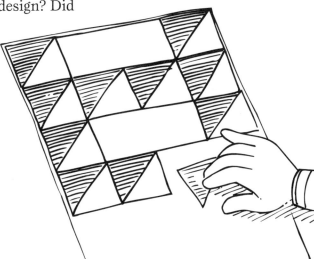

KEY EXPERIENCES

Geometry & space (Math)—

- Building complex shapes by putting simple shapes together
- Constructing with 2-d shapes

Language, symbols, & graphing (Math)—

- Making pictures and diagrams showing 1-to-1 correspondence

MATERIALS

- Pattern blocks
- Die-cut shapes (or stickers) in the same shapes and colors as the pattern blocks
- Construction paper
- Glue

EXTENSIONS

- Have children count the number of each shape used in their design.

MODIFICATIONS

- Have students create a design or pattern with the blocks or paper shapes only (that is, do not have them reproduce the original on paper).

I SPY SHAPES

STORY

Round Is a Mooncake: A Book of Shapes by Roseanne Thong

WORKSHOP SUMMARY

Students write and illustrate a shape book. This activity is child-directed and can be completed by following the student instructions.

INSTRUCTIONS

1. Each member of the group takes a copy of the "I Spy" handout.

2. Each child chooses one shape, a circle, square, triangle, or rectangle, and writes it in the blank on the handout to finish the phrase "I Spy a _____." Children can refer to the Shape handout for assistance in spelling.

3. In the center of the page, the child draws the chosen shape in black crayon.

4. The children then draws a picture around the shape, using the shape in the design. For example, a rectangle could be a door on a house.

5. At the bottom of the page, the child completes the sentence "It is a _____" (door).

6. Bind the children's pages into an *I Spy Shapes* book. Share with the class.

ASSESSMENT

- Check each child's creativity and correct portrayal of the object's shape.

EXTENSIONS

- Ask children which shape they believe is the most interesting, friendly, mean, happy, etc.

- Have children use more than one shape in a picture.

- Have children look for shapes in a "hidden picture" page.

KEY EXPERIENCES

Writing (Language & literacy)—

- Writing in specific content areas

- Acquiring, strengthening, and extending writing skills

Geometry & space (Math)—

- Identifying simple shapes within complex shapes

MATERIALS

- *Round Is a Mooncake: A Book of Shapes* by Roseanne Thong

- "I Spy" handout, p. 31 (one per child)

- "Shapes" handout, p. 32 (one or two per group)

- Black crayon

- Markers, crayons, or colored pencils

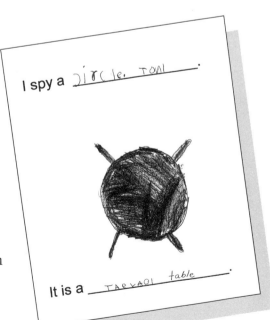

I spy a ☐iᴦᴄle. ᴛoᴎⅼ _____.

It is a ___ᴛᴀᴇᴋᴀoⅼ table_____.

MODIFICATIONS

- Have cutout shapes available for students to glue on their page.

- Have the group brainstorm ideas for their drawings before beginning the workshop.

*The student who made the drawing on the left wrote the Navajo word for **clock**, an example of something in the room in the shape of a circle.*

Name _____

I SPY

I spy a _____.

It is a _____.

SHAPES

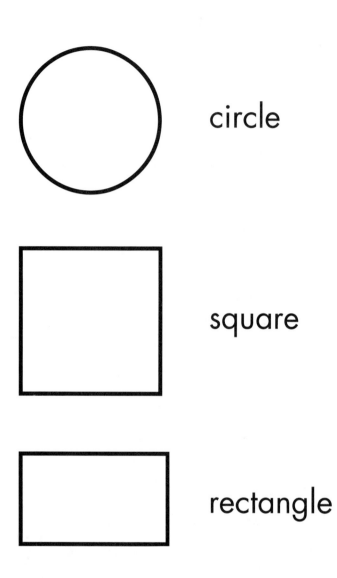

circle

square

rectangle

triangle

COMPUTER SHAPES

COMPUTER PROGRAM

Millie's Math House

WORKSHOP SUMMARY

Students create pictures using shapes with the computer program *Millie's Math House* by Edmark, either by following a blueprint or by designing their own. Children print their creations, color them, and write about them. This workshop is child-directed.

INSTRUCTIONS

1. Children work in pairs to explore the shape activity in the program.

2. After initial exploration, children choose a pattern to follow. They may also design their own picture using the shapes.

3. Children work together to move the shapes to make a picture or a design.

4. Children print their picture or design and color it.

5. Children write or dictate a sentence about their picture or design.

6. Display the shape pictures and writings in the computer area.

ASSESSMENT

- Take anecdotal notes of children's interactions with the program and with one another.

- Observe whether children are able to follow the pattern they choose or display creativity in designing their own pictures. If they design their own, did they have a plan for it and follow the plan?

- Note how children describe their pictures. Do they use the shape names? Do they include details?

KEY EXPERIENCES

Geometry & space (Math)—

- Naming simple shapes

- Sorting by shape and size

- Constructing with 2-d shapes; recognizing like shapes

- Determining shape equivalence by fitting objects together

- Building complex shapes by putting simple shapes together

MATERIALS

- *Millie's Math House* by Edmark

- Computers

- Printer

- Crayons, marker, pencil

EXTENSIONS

- This program is designed for varying levels of development; encourage children to continue to explore and make more intricate designs and pictures.

MODIFICATIONS

- Use physical adaptations to the computer as necessary.

- Work with individual children on the program as necessary until they are successful.

SINGING ABOUT SHAPES

SONG

"Shape Song," p. 36

WORKSHOP SUMMARY

Students learn a shape song and act out the movements. This activity is teacher-facilitated.

INSTRUCTIONS (TEACHER-FACILITATED)

1. Give each child a shape card. Make sure the children know what shape they have.

2. Sing the "Shape Song" for the class so children become familiar with it. The song is sung to the tune of "Twinkle, Twinkle, Little Star."

3. As a group, sing the "Shape Song." Children perform the action that accompanies their shape.

4. Ask children to suggest new actions or shapes for the song.

ASSESSMENT

• Note whether children perform the action specified for their shape.

EXTENSIONS

• Make a new song by changing the words and the tune.

MODIFICATIONS

• Substitute nonlocomotor movements (wave hands in the air, clap hands, stomp feet, nod head).

KEY EXPERIENCES

Movement—
• Acting upon movement directions
• Moving in locomotor ways

Geometry & space (Math)—
• Recognizing like shapes

MATERIALS
• "Shape Song," p. 36
• Shape cards, p. 37 (one per child)

Varying the directions in the song, the students who are holding circles walk in a circle together.

SHAPE SONG

Everyone with a circle stand up,
Hop around and then sit down.
(Sing three times to complete the tune.)

Everyone with a triangle stand up,
Turn around and then sit down.

Everyone with a rectangle stand up,
Run around and then sit down.

Everyone with a square stand up,
Skip around and then sit down.

Circle, triangle, rectangle, square;
We see shapes to compare.
(Sing once.)

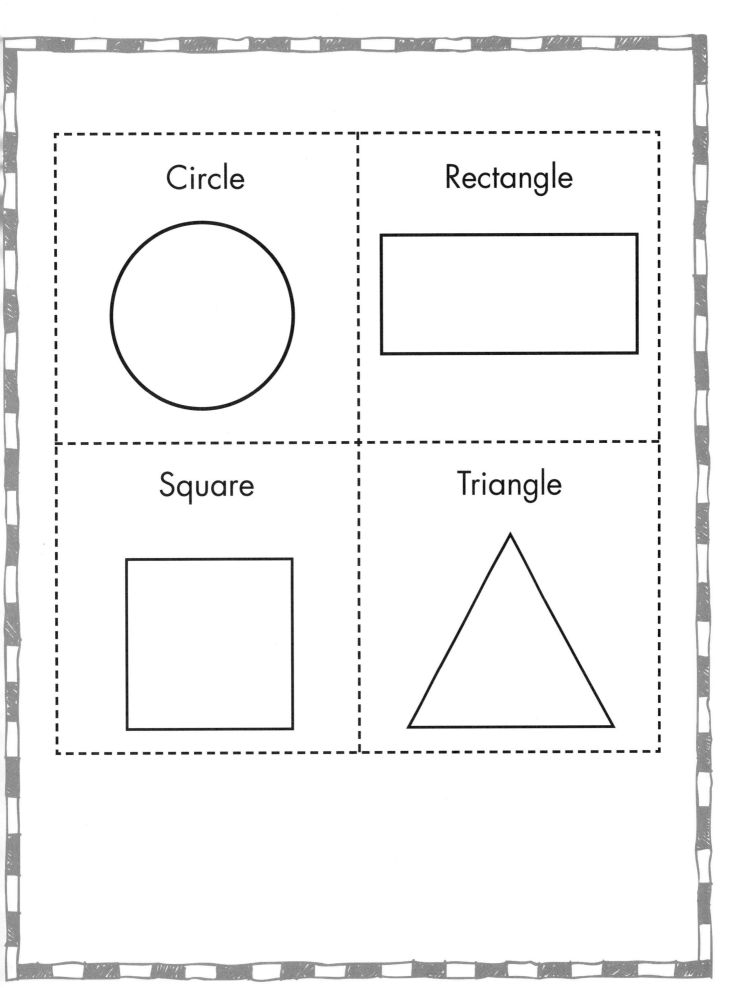

Circle

Rectangle

Square

Triangle

I SPY A SHAPE RESOURCE LIST

Burns, Marilyn. (1994). *The greedy triangle.* New York: Scholastic, Inc.

Carle, Eric. (1987). *The very hungry caterpillar.* New York: Philomel Books.

Emberley, Ed. (2001). *The wing on a flea: A book about shapes.* Little, Brown & Co.

Hoban, Tana. (1986). *Shapes, shapes, shapes.* New York: Greenwillow Books.

Hoban, Tana. (2000). *Cubes, cones, cylinders, and spheres.* New York: Greenwillow.

Jumpstart kindergarten. (1996). Knowledge Adventure.

Millie's math house. Edmark Corporation.

Reasoner, Charles. (1997). *Shapes for lunch!* New York: Price Stern Sloan, Inc.

Rogers, Paul. (1989). *The shapes game.* New York: Henry Holt and Company. (This book is out of print, but you may be able to find a copy in your school or local library.)

Thong, Roseanne. (2000). *Round is a mooncake: A book about shapes.* San Francisco: Chronicle Books.

1, 2, 3, A COUNTING SPREE!

KINDERGARTEN

1, 2, 3, A COUNTING SPREE!
Workshops at a Glance

Counting Rhyme* The group designs a rhyme counting to 12, using sets of 3. *Big Fat Hen.*	**Puppet Counting*** Students make puppets and use them to perform a counting rhyme.	**Jump-Rope Chants** Students jump rope to counting chants.
How Many Dots? Students estimate the number of dots on a piece of paper and objects in a jar, then count them. *Ten Black Dots.*	**How Many Sections?** Children compare the number of sections in an orange, a grapefruit, a tangerine, a lemon, and a lime. *Each Orange Had 8 Slices: A Counting Book.*	**Counting Games: Part I*** Each group designs a board game that uses a die.
Counting Games: Part II Groups play the games they designed in the previous workshop, as well as games created by the other groups.	**Counting on Critters** Student make a counting critter. *The Icky Bug Counting Book.*	**Our Own Counting Book*** Students choose a theme for a counting book, brainstorm related items, and create the book. *Anno's Counting Book.*

*Requires direct teacher involvement during all or part of the workshop

The workshops in this section give children a variety of enjoyable counting experiences. They revolve around five books and several rhymes and fingerplays. The story *Ten Black Dots* (Donald Crews), which introduces the workshops, explores what 10 black dots can do: "One dot can make a sun or moon when the day is done. Two dots can make the eyes of a fox. . . ." *Anno's Counting Book,* a wordless picture book by Mitsumasa Anno, uses illustrations to explore the concept of counting on different levels. Each page features the same scene of a countryside and a numeral from 1 to 10; objects are added to the scene in amounts that correspond to the numeral featured. The counting rhyme "One, two, buckle my shoe" is the text for Keith Baker's delightful *Big Fat Hen;* the rhyme is acted out by a hen and her chicks. Children will find a wealth of ideas for making their own "critters" from reading *The Icky Bug Counting Book* by Jerry Pallotta. Students will also enjoy trying to solve the word problems in Paul Giganti's *Each Orange Had 8 Slices.* Some of the workshops here utilize traditional counting rhymes and fingerplays, such as *Five Little Ducks* and *Five Little Monkeys,* and jump-rope chants.

Children's counting skills will be extended by their use of a variety of manipulatives and common objects (including some tasty fruits!). They will also have opportunities to display their counting knowledge by creating a counting book, rhyme, and board game. The jump-rope workshop, combining movement with counting, will help children realize that objects are not the only "things" that can be counted—they can also count the number of jumps they make. Other things to count include the number of steps it takes to get from the window to the door, the number of times they've been to Grandma's, and the number of days until their birthday.

Four of the workshops in this section are teacher-facilitated, and a whole-group introductory lesson starts the unit off by letting children make their own page for a class book modeled after *Ten Black Dots.*

1, 2, 3, A COUNTING SPREE!
Whole-Group Introductory Lesson

MATERIALS

- *Ten Black Dots* by Donald Crews
- Die-cut black dots (10 per child)
- Construction paper, any size and color (one sheet per child)
- Large sheet of newsprint
- Marker or pen
- Glue
- Crayons or markers

INSTRUCTIONS

Read the story *Ten Black Dots* by Donald Crews to the class. This short story shows what can be made by using 1 dot, 2 dots, and so on, all the way through 10 dots. Discuss with the class how the dots were used.

With the children's help, make a list of other ways dots could be used. Number 1–10 down the side of the newsprint. Beside each number, write down the children's ideas of what they could make with that number of dots. For instance, 1 dot could be the steering wheel on a car; 2 dots, Mickey Mouse's ears.

Give each child a piece of construction paper and 10 black dots. Explain that children will design a picture using as many of the black dots as they like. Children may use the ideas brainstormed by the class or come up with their own. Encourage children to spend some time arranging and rearranging their dots until they are satisfied with the picture they want to make.

Give children glue and crayons or markers to complete their pictures. Bind the pages into a class book and place it somewhere for everyone to look at.

Two dots make a tiger's eyes!

COUNTING RHYME

STORY

Big Fat Hen by Keith Baker

WORKSHOP SUMMARY

The group designs a rhyme counting to 12, using sets of 3. This activity is teacher-facilitated.

INSTRUCTIONS (TEACHER-FACILITATED)

1. Share the book *Big Fat Hen* with the group. As children look at the illustrations, help them discover that the bugs correspond with one number on the page and the eggs with the other number on the page.

2. Discuss the pattern the author uses to create the rhyme. Help children see that the rhyme is formed by using the last number in the series (2, 4, 6, etc.). Ask students to point out the words that rhyme in the story.

3. Explain that the group is going to write a counting rhyme that counts to the number 12. It will be similar to the rhyme in the book, but instead of having a rhyming word after every two numbers, it will have a rhyming word after every three numbers. On a large piece of paper, write the numbers 1–12. With children's help, circle every third number (3, 6, 9, 12). These are the numbers the group will need to think of rhyming words for. Brainstorm a list of words rhyming with these four numbers and write these down.

4. Ask children how they could make each number and its rhyming word into a sentence (for example, "One, two, three, come count with me").

5. When the rhyme is completed, practice it with the group and then perform for the class.

ASSESSMENT

- Note children's ability to think of appropriate rhyming words.

- Look for creativity in creating the rhyme.

EXTENSIONS

- Have children act out or illustrate the new rhyme.

- Make a counting rhyme with a number larger than 12 or using different groupings of numbers.

- Have students count all the chicks on the last page of the story.

KEY EXPERIENCES

Speaking & listening (Language & literacy)—

- Participating in singing, story-telling, poetic, and dramatic activities

Number & numerical operations (Math)—

- Using the words "one, two, three, …" in consistent order when attempting to count beyond small sets

Writing (Language & literacy)—

- Writing in specific content areas

MATERIALS

- *Big Fat Hen* by Keith Baker
- Paper
- Pencil

MODIFICATIONS

- Make a list of words that rhyme with 2, 4, 6, 8 to model the rhyming process, then ask children to come up with the rhyming words for 3, 6, 9, 12.

- Provide a list of words (or pictures) that rhyme with the numbers; students choose from these words to compose the rhyme.

TREE

BEE   KNEE

ME

1, 2, 3, a bee stung me!

PUPPET COUNTING

RHYMES/FINGERPLAYS

"Five Little Ducks," "Five Little Monkeys," "Five Little Pumpkins," "Five Green & Speckled Frogs"

WORKSHOP SUMMARY

Students make puppets and use them to perform a counting rhyme. This activity is teacher-facilitated and will require more than one workshop period.

INSTRUCTIONS (TEACHER-FACILITATED)

1. Assign each group a different rhyme from pp. 47–50. (For additional rhymes look in fingerplay books, such as *Finger Frolics,* by Liz Cromwell and Dixie Hibner.) If students are unfamiliar with the rhyme, go through it with them a few times until they are comfortable with it.

2. Explain that they will be making puppets to act out their rhyme. Discuss the puppets they think they will need (such as frogs, bugs, ducks, monkeys, doctor, etc.) and perhaps some props.

3. Ask the group to decide on the type of puppets they would like to make: paper bag, popsicle stick, paper plate, or some other kind. All members of the group will design the same type. You may wish to have each group create a different type.

4. Provide materials for children to make the puppets.

5. Have students practice the rhyme using their puppets.

6. Have students perform for the class.

ASSESSMENT

- Videotape the groups as they perform. Let them watch the tape and assess their performance.

KEY EXPERIENCES

Speaking & listening (Language & literacy)—

- Participating in singing, storytelling, poetic, and dramatic activities

Number & numerical operations (Math)—

- Recognizing or counting small sets

Language, symbols, & graphing (Math)—

- Using words, pictures, and models to represent experiences with collecting, sorting, counting, constructing, pouring, and moving

MATERIALS

- Counting rhymes, pp. 47–50
- Variety of art materials

EXTENSIONS

- Make a new rhyme.

- Perform for another class or grade level.

- Get as creative with this workshop as you like. For instance, one class hosted a "premiere party." They made props along with their puppets and made signs introducing the plays and the performers. They sent out a "press release," and the movie "opened" during parent-teacher conferences. On opening day they dressed up, put out a red carpet for the "stars," and ate popcorn while enjoying the show.

MODIFICATIONS

- Have students use classroom puppets rather than make their own.

- Use rhymes children are already familiar with.

BACKGROUND READING

- Christelow, Eileen. *Five Little Monkeys Jumping on the Bed.* 1989. New York: Houghton Mifflin.

- *Five Little Ducks: Raffi Songs to Read.* 1989. Illustrated by José Aruego and Ariane Dewey. New York: Crown Publishers, Inc.

This group of students made five stick puppets and a hill to perform "Five Little Ducks" for the rest of the class.

Five Little Ducks

Five little ducks went out to play,

Over the hill and far away.

Mother Duck said, "Quack, quack, quack."

Four little ducks came waddling back.

Four little ducks went out to play,

Over the hill and far away.

Mother Duck said, "Quack, quack, quack."

Three little ducks came waddling back.

Three little ducks went out to play,

Over the hill and far away.

Mother Duck said, "Quack, quack, quack."

Two little ducks came waddling back.

Two little ducks went out to play,

Over the hill and far away.

Mother Duck said, "Quack, quack, quack."

One little duck came waddling back.

One little duck went out to play,

Over the hill and far away.

Mother Duck said, "Quack, quack, quack."

No little ducks came waddling back.

No little ducks went out to play,

Over the hill and far away.

Father Duck said, "QUACK, QUACK, QUACK."

Five little ducks came waddling back.

Five Little Monkeys

Five little monkeys jumping on the bed,
One fell off and bumped his head.
Mama called the doctor and the doctor said,
"No more monkeys jumping on the bed!"
Four little monkeys jumping on the bed,
One fell off and bumped his head.
Mama called the doctor and the doctor said,
"No more monkeys jumping on the bed!"
Three little monkeys jumping on the bed,
One fell off and bumped his head.
Mama called the doctor and the doctor said,
"No more monkeys jumping on the bed!"
Two little monkeys jumping on the bed,
One fell off and bumped his head.
Mama called the doctor and the doctor said,
"No more monkeys jumping on the bed!"
One little monkey jumping on the bed,
He fell off and bumped his head.
Mama called the doctor and the doctor said,
"NO MORE MONKEYS JUMPING ON THE BED!"

Five Little Pumpkins

Five little pumpkins sitting on a gate,

The first one said, "Oh my, it's getting late."

The second one said, "There are witches in the air!"

The third one said, "I don't care."

The fourth one said, "Let's run and run and run!"

The fifth one said, "I'm ready for some fun!"

Then "BOO!" went the witch,

and out went the lights,

And five little pumpkins rolled out of sight.

Five Green and Speckled Frogs

Five green and speckled frogs
Sat on a speckled log,
Eating some most delicious bugs—yum, yum!
One jumped into the pool,
Where it was nice and cool,
Now there are four green speckled frogs—glub, glub!
Four green and speckled frogs
Sat on a speckled log,
Eating some most delicious bugs—yum, yum!
One jumped into the pool,
Where it was nice and cool,
Now there are three green speckled frogs—glub, glub!
Three green and speckled frogs
Sat on a speckled log,
Eating some most delicious bugs—yum, yum!
One jumped into the pool,
Where it was nice and cool,
Now there are two green speckled frogs—glub, glub!
Two green and speckled frogs
Sat on a speckled log,
Eating some most delicious bugs—yum, yum!
One jumped into the pool,
Where it was nice and cool,
Now there is one green speckled frog—glub, glub!
One green and speckled frog
Sat on a speckled log,
Eating some most delicious bugs—yum, yum!
He jumped into the pool,
Where it was nice and cool,
Now there are no green speckled frogs—glub, glub!

This is a reproducible page.

JUMP-ROPE CHANTS

WORKSHOP SUMMARY

Students jump rope to counting chants. This workshop is child-directed and can be completed by following the student instructions.

INSTRUCTIONS

Before beginning this activity, you may want to teach the chants to the entire class.

1. Children choose a jump-rope chant, such as "Teddy Bear, Teddy Bear," "Cinderella," or "Bubble Gum, Bubble Gum." (For other ideas, see books such as *Anna Banana: 101 Jump-Rope Rhymes* by Joanna Cole.)

2. A student jumps a rope while the rest of the group chants.

3. After the chant, the group counts the number of times the student is able to jump the rope.

4. One child records the number of jumps for each student.

5. When everyone has had a turn, the children line up according to the number of jumps they made.

ASSESSMENT

- Note whether children line up accurately, based on the number of jumps they recorded.

EXTENSIONS

- Make a class graph recording how many students jumped a certain number of times.

- Have students create a new jump-rope chant.

MODIFICATIONS

- Have children hop or jump in place instead of jump rope. This can be done as a group or individually.

KEY EXPERIENCES

Movement—
- Feeling and expressing steady beat
- Moving in locomotor ways

Number & numerical operations (Math)—
- Using one word for each item counted, when counting beyond small sets

MATERIALS

- Small jump ropes
- Jump-rope chants, p. 52
- Paper
- Pencil

JUMP-ROPE CHANTS

Cinderella

Cinderella dressed in yella'

Went upstairs to kiss her fella,

Made a mistake and kissed a snake,

How many doctors did it take?

Bubble Gum

Bubble gum, bubble gum, in a dish,

How many pieces do you wish?

Teddy Bear, Teddy Bear

Teddy Bear, Teddy Bear,

Touch the ground.

Teddy Bear, Teddy Bear,

Turn around.

Teddy Bear, Teddy Bear,

Go upstairs.

Teddy Bear, Teddy Bear,

Say your prayers.

Teddy Bear, Teddy Bear,

Turn off the light.

Teddy Bear, Teddy Bear,

Say "Good night."

This is a reproducible page.

HOW MANY DOTS?

STORY

Ten Black Dots by Donald Crews

WORKSHOP SUMMARY

Students estimate the number of dots on a piece of paper and objects in a jar, then count them. Children complete the workshop by following the student instructions.

INSTRUCTIONS

1. Give each group a piece of dot paper.

2. Before counting the dots, each student guesses how many there are and writes his or her estimate on the back of the dot paper.

3. Students count the dots and write the actual number underneath the dots.

4. Students discuss whether their estimates were higher or lower than the actual number.

5. Next the children look at the jar of objects. Each child writes his or her estimate of the number of objects in the jar on the sheet of paper.

6. The children pour the objects out and count them.

7. They determine which child's estimate was closest to the actual number of objects.

ASSESSMENT

- Observe the way children estimate and note how close they come to the actual number of objects.

EXTENSIONS

- Have students connect the dots on the page to make a design.

- Provide materials such as stickers or stamps for children to make their own estimation sheets, like the one with the dots.

KEY EXPERIENCES

Number & numerical operations (Math)—

- Using the words "one, two, three, …" in consistent order when attempting to count beyond small sets

- Using one word for each item counted, when counting beyond small sets

Language, symbols, & graphing (Math)—

- Recognizing and writing numerals and counting words

MATERIALS

- Dot paper, p. 55 (one per child)

- Pencil

- Paper (one sheet per group)

- Jar of pennies, marbles, or manipulatives

- Provide a plastic jar for children to take home, fill, and bring back for the class to estimate the number of objects in it. (Be sure the child knows how many items are in the jar and tells you.)

- Encourage students to look around the room or school for other things they can estimate—for example, the number of tiles on the ceiling, the number of boots lined up near the door, the number of steps on a stairway, etc.

MODIFICATIONS

- Have children draw a line through each dot as it is counted so that it will not be recounted.

- Write the groups' estimates on the board for children to copy onto their paper.

Name _____

[Handout 1: How Many Dots?]

HOW MANY SECTIONS?

STORY

Each Orange Had 8 Slices: A Counting Book by Paul Giganti, Jr.

WORKSHOP SUMMARY

Children compare the number of sections in an orange, a grapefruit, a tangerine, a lemon, and a lime. Children complete the activity by following the student instructions.

INSTRUCTIONS

You may wish to have the children experience peeling the fruit themselves during a mini-lesson before the workshop. Some students may need assistance. You may also want to read part or all of the story to the class. During the workshop, the children will explore the answer to one of the word problems presented in the story.

1. Each student chooses a fruit and places it on a paper plate.

2. Each child takes a Fruit Section handout and fills in the first blank, indicating what type of fruit he or she has.

3. Each child guesses how many sections (or pieces) the fruit has and records the estimate on the group recording chart. (You may need to explain the term *section* to the groups.) Ask students if they think each fruit of the same type will have the same number of sections.

4. Each child breaks his or her fruit into sections and counts the number of sections.

5. The child records the number of sections on the handout and on the group recording chart.

6. Students use the appropriate color of crayon to draw the number of fruit sections on their handout.

7. Children discuss how close their estimates were and which types of fruit had the most and least number of sections. Students place their handouts in order from the least to the greatest number of sections.

8. Children taste the different types of fruit.

ASSESSMENT

- Check the order of the handouts for accuracy.
- Check the pictures for the correct number of sections.

KEY EXPERIENCES

Collections of objects (Math)—

- Comparing collections 1-to-1; determining "more," "less," "the same as"

Number & numerical operations (Math)—

- Using one word for each item counted, when counting beyond small sets

Language, symbols, & graphing (Math)—

- Using words, pictures, and models to represent experiences with counting

MATERIALS

- *Each Orange Had 8 Slices* by Paul Giganti, Jr.
- One (or two) orange, grapefruit, tangerine, lemon, lime per group (peeled)
- Orange, yellow, and green crayons
- "Fruit Sections" handout, p. 58 (one per student)
- "How Many Sections?" chart, p. 59 (one per group)
- Napkins, paper towels, or paper plates

EXTENSIONS

- Have students compare their numbers with those of other groups to see if all oranges have the same number of sections, all lemons have the same, etc. Ask them to draw some conclusions about the number of sections that may be found in each type of fruit.

- Discuss the different tastes of the fruit, such as sweet and sour.

- Have children chart the information on a class or group picture graph.

- Have students count the seeds in the fruits and compare the different types. Have them add this information to their handouts.

- Assist students in writing a number sentence showing the total number of sections the group has.

MODIFICATIONS

- Have the fruit peeled and sectioned ahead of time.

FRUIT SECTIONS

My fruit is a _____.

It has _____ sections.

HOW MANY SECTIONS?

	Guess	Count
Orange		
Grapefruit		
Tangerine		
Lemon		
Lime		

[Handout 2: How Many Sections?]

COUNTING GAMES: PART I

WORKSHOP SUMMARY

Each group designs a board game that uses a die. This workshop is teacher-facilitated.

INSTRUCTIONS (TEACHER-FACILITATED)

This activity may take more than one workshop period to complete.

1. Show the group the game Candy Land and point out how the path is made of different colors of squares. Ask the children if they know of other board games that have paths.

2. Explain that the group is going to make a game of their own. Show them the squares they will use to make their path, and help them work together to arrange and glue the squares on the poster board or tag board. Their path should have 20–30 squares.

3. Once the path is complete, have the students write (or copy) *Start* and *End* at the appropriate spots. Or, they can draw a picture showing the beginning and end of the path.

4. Provide stickers, markers, and stamps for the children to make their game board interesting and colorful. The group may want to decide on a theme and/or a name for their game. Help them brainstorm some ideas.

5. Explain that in another workshop (see p. 62), children will actually play their game and have a chance to play the other groups' games as well. Students will be rolling a die and moving their manipulative or game piece the corresponding number of spaces. But before playing the game, have the children decide on some rules, such as who begins and what to do if two players land on the same spot.

6. Write these rules down so students can refer to them as they play their game. They may find that they need to modify or add some rules as they begin playing.

7. Have children choose a die and manipulatives or game pieces to go with their game.

ASSESSMENT

- Note how children work together as they create their game. How do they decide on a path? How do they develop the rules for the game? Do they use any ideas from games they are already familiar with?

KEY EXPERIENCES

Number & numerical operations (Math)—

- Using the words "one, two, three, …" in consistent order when attempting to count beyond small sets
- Using one word for each item counted, when counting beyond small sets

MATERIALS

- Candy Land or other board game with a path
- Poster board or tag board
- Die-cut squares (20–30 small per group)
- Glue
- Stickers, markers, stamps
- Dice
- Manipulatives or game pieces

EXTENSIONS

- Encourage children to bring in board games from home.

- Encourage students to add directions on their path, such as "Go back 1 space" and "Go forward 3 spaces." These may be indicated by a + and – sign: " + 3," "–1." Dots may be substituted for numerals: " + •••," "– •."

MODIFICATIONS

- Give students the option of drawing their game path rather than using the die-cut squares.

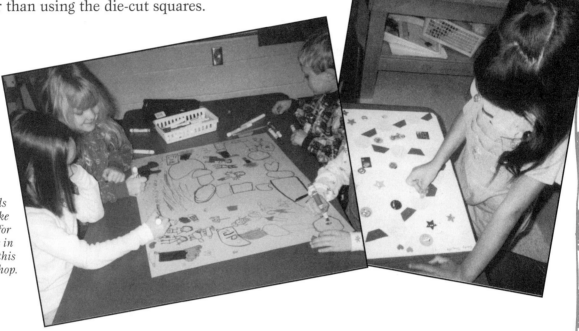

The game boards students make can be used for other activities in addition to this workshop.

COUNTING GAMES: PART II

WORKSHOP SUMMARY

Groups play the games they designed in the previous workshop, as well as games created by the other groups. This is a student-directed workshop.

KEY EXPERIENCES

Number & numerical operations (Math)—

- Using the words "one, two, three, …" in consistent order when attempting to count beyond small sets
- Using one word for each item counted, when counting beyond small sets

MATERIALS

- Student-made game boards from *Counting Games: Part I* workshop
- Dice
- Manipulatives or game pieces

INSTRUCTIONS

1. Have all of the groups' game boards available. Students choose a game to play in pairs or with the whole group.

2. Students play the game, following any rules or instructions included. Any questions they have about a game created by another group may be referred to that group.

ASSESSMENT

- Assess each game's "playability."

- Take anecdotal notes of cooperation and group interactions.

- Note how children deal with questions that arise about the instructions or rules for the games they created.

EXTENSIONS

- Encourage children to modify the game boards to make the games easier or more difficult.

- Have children use number cards instead of dice.

- Let children take turns playing the games at home and report on how their families played them.

- Have games available during plan-do-review time.

MODIFICATIONS

- If necessary, assist students in playing the games cooperatively.

COUNTING ON CRITTERS

STORY

The Icky Bug Counting Book by Jerry Pallotta

WORKSHOP SUMMARY

Students make a counting critter by adding details such as one nose, six legs, eight spots, etc. This workshop is child-directed; it can be completed by following the student instructions.

INSTRUCTIONS

1. The students look through the book and point out interesting features on the insects—for example, wings, eyes, spots, stripes, and so on. Ask the group to use the pictures to get some ideas for features they could add to their own critters.

2. Each student takes several circles and overlaps them to make a body for the critter. One circle will be for the head.

3. Children glue the circles together on the sheet of construction paper.

4. Using crayons, markers, and a variety of art materials, students add features to their critter in groups representing the numbers 1–10. For example, they might give the critter 1 nose, 2 eyes, 3 antennae, 4 teeth, 5 tails, 6 hands, 7 stars on the body, 8 feet, 9 hats, and 10 wings. You might ask questions to help students get some ideas: "What are some things you noticed on the bugs in the book? What are some silly things you could add?" Encourage students to be creative.

5. Display the finished critters. Have students name them.

KEY EXPERIENCES

Geometry & space (Math)—
- Constructing with 2-d shapes

Number & numerical operations (Math)—
- Using one word for each item counted, when counting beyond small sets

MATERIALS

- *The Icky Bug Counting Book* by Jerry Pallotta
- Construction paper circles (several per student)
- Construction paper (one sheet per student)
- Variety of art materials, including crayons & markers
- Glue

ASSESSMENT

- Observe whether students count out materials as they create their critters and whether they add the features in amounts from 1–10.

EXTENSIONS

- Have students label how many of each feature their critter has.

- Encourage children to write a story about their critter.

- Have students write statements about the critter. For example, "It has 5 eyes and 1 nose."

MODIFICATIONS

- Provide suggestions of features for children to use.

- Assist students in counting out the desired number of each feature before they glue them on or as they draw them.

OUR OWN COUNTING BOOK

STORY

Anno's Counting Book by Mitsumasa Anno

WORKSHOP SUMMARY

Students choose a theme for a counting book, brainstorm related items, and create the book. This workshop is teacher-facilitated.

INSTRUCTIONS (TEACHER-FACILITATED)

1. Look through the book with the group. The children should discover that the items in each illustration correspond with the number on that page.

2. Help the group decide on a theme for their own counting book—for example, baseball, birthday, circus, etc. Then have students brainstorm a list of items related to the theme. You might ask what items or things are involved in the activity they've chosen; ask them for 10 different things. Make a list of these and have children assign a number, 1–10, to each item; for example, if the theme is baseball they might list one ball, two bats, three gloves, and so on.

3. Give each student one or two sheets of construction paper. Once they decide who is going to draw what, they can write the number and name of their item on their paper. Avoid giving one student both the *9* and *10* pages, and assign the child with the *1* page the *9* or *10* page also to ensure that students are not overwhelmed with the amount to be drawn.

KEY EXPERIENCES

Language, symbols, & graphing (Math)—

- Recognizing and writing numerals and counting words
- Making pictures showing 1-to-1 correspondence
- Using words, pictures, and models to represent experiences with counting

MATERIALS

- *Anno's Counting Book* by Mitsumasa Anno
- Construction paper (10 sheets)
- Marker
- Variety of art materials, including markers and crayons

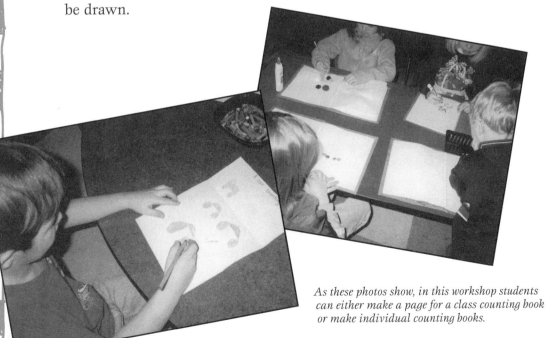

As these photos show, in this workshop students can either make a page for a class counting book or make individual counting books.

4. Students illustrate their pages with the appropriate number of items.

5. Help students decide on a title for their book. Bind it and share with the rest of the class.

ASSESSMENT

• Evaluate the books for accuracy and creativity.

EXTENSIONS

• Have each child make his or her own book.

• Make the theme of the book into a song and sing to the tune of "This Old Man."

MODIFICATIONS

• Choose the theme for the group and give only one page and item to each child.

• Have students make a book of only 5 or 6 pages instead of 10.

Students in one classroom made a counting book showing items having to do with birthdays, including three birthday guests.

1, 2, 3, A COUNTING SPREE RESOURCE LIST

Anno, Mitsumasa. (1975). *Anno's counting book.* Mexico: HarperCollins Publishers, Inc.

Baker, Keith. (1994). *Big fat hen.* New York: Harcourt Brace and Company.

Christelow, Eileen. (1989). *Five little monkeys jumping on the bed.* New York: Houghton Mifflin.

Crews, Donald. (1986). *Ten black dots.* New York: Greenwillow Books.

Five little ducks: Raffi songs to read. (1989). José Aruego and Ariane Dewey (illustrators). New York: Crown Publishers, Inc.

Giganti, Paul, Jr. (1992). *Each orange had 8 slices: A counting book.* New York: Greenwillow Books.

Pallotta, Jerry. (1992). *The icky bug counting book.* Watertown, Massachusetts: Charlesbridge Publishing.

BIG, SMALL, AND IN BETWEEN: ORDERING, COMPARING, AND MEASURING

GRADE 1

BIG, SMALL, AND IN BETWEEN: ORDERING, COMPARING, AND MEASURING
Workshops at a Glance

Note: All the workshops in this section relate to *Goldilocks and the Three Bears* by Jan Brett. Additional books are noted in the workshop descriptions below.

Bowls and Spoons* Students discover how many small, medium, and large spoonfuls of rice will fill small, medium, and large bowls.	**Beginning, Middle, and End** Students illustrate the sequence of events in their favorite part of the story.	**Greater Than, Less Than*** Students compare two numbers rolled on dice.
Jump Narrow, Jump Wide Students play "Jump the Brook" with a jump rope and measure how far they can jump.	**Which Is Tallest? Which Is Shortest?** Students build block towers and determine their order by height.	**What's Lightest, What's Heaviest?** Students weigh a variety of objects in the room, then place them in order by weight.
Great Big Bears, Little Tiny Bears Students arrange teddy bears by size.	**High Tones, Low Tones*** Students experiment with instruments to discover high and low tones.	**Lost Teeth: Most to Fewest*** Students compare the number of teeth they've lost. *How Many Teeth?*

*Requires direct teacher involvement during all or part of the workshop

The classic story of big, little, and in between, *Goldilocks and the Three Bears,* is the focus of this set of first-grade workshops. Students measure and compare objects in a variety of ways, including by length, height, width, number, weight, and musical tone. Several activities ask children to sequence or seriate objects according to these characteristics. The workshops utilize a wide variety of objects, including rice, blocks, jump ropes, dice, teddy bears, musical instruments, even teeth! In most of the workshops children also make some sort of visual display of their measurements and comparisons, such as illustrations, graphs, and arrangement of objects in order.

In addition to the Goldilocks story, *How Many Teeth?* by Paul Showers is featured in one of the workshops here. This nonfiction book takes readers through the growth and loss of teeth from infancy through adulthood.

There are four teacher-facilitated workshops in this section. A whole-group introductory lesson is also included.

BIG, SMALL, AND IN BETWEEN
Whole-Group Introductory Lesson

MATERIALS

- *Goldilocks and the Three Bears* by Jan Brett

INSTRUCTIONS

Read the story to the class, then discuss things in the story that were small, medium, and large. Ask children to look around the room and name things they see that are small, medium, and large.

Discuss the number of bears in the family in the book. Ask students to raise their hands if there are three people living in their own home. Have these children stand or sit in a group together. Then ask which students have two people in their home, and have them form another group. Continue asking who has four, five, and so on until everyone has joined a group. Have the class count the number of students in each group, and note the group that has the largest number.

BOWLS AND SPOONS

STORY

Goldilocks and the Three Bears by Jan Brett

WORKSHOP SUMMARY

Students discover how many small, medium, and large spoonfuls of rice will fill small, medium, and large bowls. This activity is teacher-facilitated.

INSTRUCTIONS (TEACHER-FACILITATED)

1. Ask students to place the bowls and spoons in order from largest to smallest. Ask the children, "Which is the largest bowl? Which is the smallest? Where would you place the last bowl?"

2. Ask students to estimate how many large spoonfuls of rice it will take to fill up the large bowl. Have them write their estimates in the appropriate column on the handout.

3. Have students take turns using the large spoon to fill the large bowl with rice. Count together as they fill the bowl.

4. Compare the estimates and the actual count. Ask students whether their estimates were correct. How much of a difference was there between the estimates and actual counts?

5. Repeat steps 2–4 with the medium spoon/bowl and the small spoon/bowl. The estimates should get more accurate.

KEY EXPERIENCES

Measurement of continuous quantity (Math)—

- Filling containers by repeated pouring from a single smaller container

Number & numerical operations (Math)—

- Using the words "one, two, three, …" in consistent order when attempting to count beyond small sets

- Using one word for each item counted, when counting beyond small sets

MATERIALS

- Small, medium, and large bowls
- Small, medium, and large spoons
- Rice
- "Bowls and Spoons" handout, p. 75 (one per student)
- Marker

ASSESSMENT

- Note children's attempts at estimation, looking for more accuracy with each estimate.

- Take anecdotal notes on how children order the objects according to size and how accurately they count and measure.

EXTENSIONS

- Have students experiment with filling each bowl with each different-sized spoon. They can record their estimates and actual measurements on a chart similar to the one shown at right.

- Have students use one size spoon to fill each bowl, then make a picture graph showing how many spoonfuls it took to fill each size bowl.

- Have students use pitchers and glasses of various sizes to perform the same experiment with liquid.

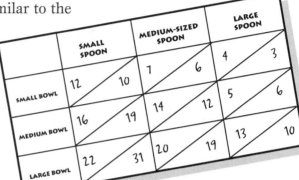

	SMALL SPOON		MEDIUM-SIZED SPOON		LARGE SPOON	
SMALL BOWL	12	10	7	6	4	3
MEDIUM BOWL	16	19	14	12	5	6
LARGE BOWL	22	31	20	19	13	10

MODIFICATIONS

- Provide prior opportunities for children to work with estimation.

Name _____

BOWLS AND SPOONS

	SMALL 	MEDIUM 	LARGE 
ESTIMATE			
ACTUAL NUMBER			

[Handout 1: Bowls and Spoons]

BEGINNING, MIDDLE, AND END

STORY

Goldilocks and the Three Bears

WORKSHOP SUMMARY

Students illustrate the sequence of events in their favorite part of the story. This activity is student-directed and can be completed by following the student instructions.

INSTRUCTIONS

1. The group splits into two groups. One group sequences the picture cards from the story. The other group (or one to two children, depending on computer availability) uses the program *Sammy's Science House: Make a Movie* on the computer. In this program children place the pictures on the screen in order and watch the movie that follows from this.

2. Each child takes a 6" × 18" strip of construction paper that has been folded into thirds. On the strip, the children illustrate their favorite part of *Goldilocks*. They need to show the sequence of their favorite part, including the beginning, middle, and end.

ASSESSMENT

- Note whether children successfully sequence the cards. Ask them to tell you, using the pictures on the cards, what happened at the beginning, what happened in the middle, and finally what happened at the end.

KEY EXPERIENCES

Speaking & listening (Language & literacy)—
- Recalling thoughts and observations in a purposeful context

Language, symbols, & graphing (Math)—
- Creating timelines
- Using "first, second, third, ..." to describe position

MATERIALS
- Sequence cards, p. 78
- Computers
- Computer program *Sammy's Science House* by Edmark
- 6" × 18" strip of construction paper, folded into thirds (one for each student)
- Variety of art materials

- Observe children using the *Sammy's Science House* program.
- Check for understanding of *beginning, middle,* and *end* in children's illustrated sequences.

EXTENSIONS

- Have students design an illustrated sequence for another favorite story.
- Make a movie using *HyperStudio* or *KidPix* computer programs.
- Ask parents to send in three or four pictures of their child at various ages. Have children sequence these from infancy to their current age.

MODIFICATIONS

- Have students look at the book while sequencing and while illustrating.

GREATER THAN, LESS THAN

STORY

Goldilocks and the Three Bears

WORKSHOP SUMMARY

Students compare two numbers rolled on dice. This activity is teacher-facilitated.

INSTRUCTIONS (TEACHER-FACILITATED)

Before beginning this workshop, create a blank number line on each construction paper strip. Draw a 12-inch line using the ruler and divide this line into 2-inch sections. Be sure to mark the beginning and end of the line also.

If your students are not familiar with the symbols >, <, and =, go over the meanings with them beforehand. You may also want to post a reference sheet nearby during the actual workshop.

1. Give each child a blank number line.

2. Have each child add numbers to the number line, beginning with 0 and ending with 6. Ask "What number should the number line begin with? What is the largest number we can count on one die? That number will end the number line."

3. Once the number lines are ready, have a child roll the dice. Ask the child to count the number of dots on one of the dice, and have each child place a manipulative on that number on his or her number line. Each also writes the number on the handout under the "1st roll" column.

4. The second die is then counted, and a different manipulative is placed on the number line at that number. Have children place the > or < card between the two numbers (or the = card if both numbers were the same). Then have them write the second number under the "2nd roll" column on the handout.

5. In the last column on the handout, have children write comparative statements using the greater than, less than, or equal signs. For example, if a 3 and 5 were rolled, the children would write the following statements: *3 < 5, 5 > 3.*

KEY EXPERIENCES

Numbers & numerical operations (Math)—

- Comparing two numbers
- Using the words "one, two, three, …" in consistent order when attempting to count beyond small sets

Language, symbols, & graphing (Math)—

- Creating number lines

MATERIALS

- 2 dice
- >, <, = cards, p. 81
- Ruler
- Pencil
- 2" × 18" strip of construction paper (one per child)
- "Greater Than, Less Than" handout, p. 82 (one per child)
- Manipulatives

6. Have another child roll the dice, and continue from step 3.

7. Repeat these steps using three dice, and compare all three numbers.

ASSESSMENT

- Check for understanding and correct usage of the symbols.

- Note how children use the number line.

EXTENSIONS

- Have students compare the two numbers without using the number line and manipulatives.

MODIFICATIONS

- None needed.

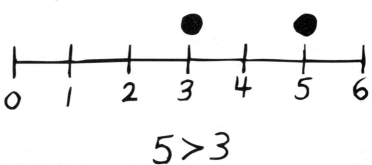

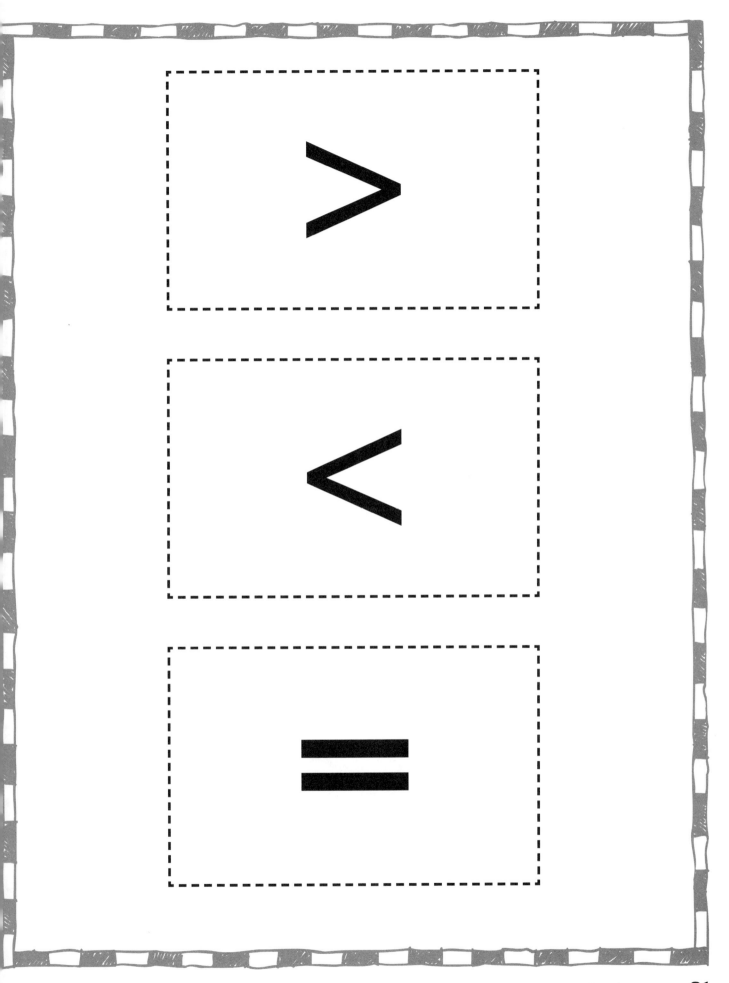

Name _____

> GREATER THAN   < LESS THAN

	1st roll	2nd roll	> < =
1.	_____	_____	_____
2.	_____	_____	_____
3.	_____	_____	_____
4.	_____	_____	_____
5.	_____	_____	_____
6.	_____	_____	_____
7.	_____	_____	_____
8.	_____	_____	_____
9.	_____	_____	_____
10.	_____	_____	_____
11.	_____	_____	_____
12.	_____	_____	_____
13.	_____	_____	_____
14.	_____	_____	_____
15.	_____	_____	_____

[Handout 1: Greater Than, Less Than]

This is a reproducible page.

JUMP NARROW, JUMP WIDE

STORY

Goldilocks and the Three Bears

WORKSHOP SUMMARY

Students play "Jump the Brook" with a jump rope and measure how far they can jump. They complete the activity by following the student instructions.

INSTRUCTIONS

Before beginning this workshop, set up an area in the classroom, hallway, or outdoors where children can jump over the ropes. To set up the game, tape one of the jump ropes to the floor. Using the ruler, measure 12 inches and put a tape line where the second jump rope will be laid. Continue this procedure five or six more times so that five to six taped lines are laid, each 12 inches apart.

Discuss with children the meaning of the terms *narrow* and *wide* if they are not familiar with them.

1. The children lay the second jump rope on the first tape line. They form a line and "jump the brook" (two jump ropes).

2. The students move the second jump rope to the next tape line and again try to jump the brook, starting from the first jump rope.

KEY EXPERIENCES

Movement—
- Moving in locomotor ways

Movement, time, & speed (Math)—
- Moving along pathways involving straight and curved lines

MATERIALS

- Two jump ropes
- Ruler
- Tape
- Measuring objects, such as string, paper clips, or blocks

3. They continue moving the jump rope and jumping across until they cannot make it over the brook. Children can sit out as they are unable to jump both of the ropes, leaving one person as the winner, or at each new width every child can attempt to jump the brook.

4. Children write their name on a piece of tape and put it next to the farthest line they were able to jump over.

5. Students measure their jumping distance with string, paper clips, or blocks.

ASSESSMENT

• Note whether children use the terms *narrow* and *wide*. Ask who jumped the widest brook and who jumped the narrowest brook.

• Assess children's measurements of their jumps.

EXTENSIONS

• Students try to flick plastic circles or jumping frogs across the brook.

• Ask students to suggest a replacement for the "brook" they are jumping over—a pit of lava, snakes, etc.

MODIFICATIONS

• Have children toss a bean bag instead of jump.

• Provide a chore or task to keep children who sit out early in the game involved, such as counting jumps or keeping score.

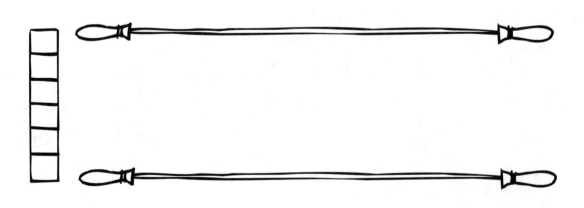

Miranda jumped 6 blocks.

WHICH IS TALLEST? WHICH IS SHORTEST?

STORY

Goldilocks and the Three Bears

WORKSHOP SUMMARY

Students build block towers and determine their order by height. Children complete the activity by following the student instructions.

INSTRUCTIONS

1. Each child builds a tower of blocks or cubes.

2. Children compare the height of each tower and, on a sheet of paper, write the names of the builders in order according to the height of their towers.

3. Children fill in the Block Tower Graph for each tower made. They can color in the number of squares corresponding to the number of blocks in the towers, or they can glue the corresponding number of die-cut squares on the graph.

ASSESSMENT

- Check the accuracy of the graphs.

- Ask whose tower was the tallest and whose was the shortest. How did they order the rest of the towers?

KEY EXPERIENCES

Measurement of continuous quantity (Math)—
- Comparing lengths by side-by-side matching

Geometry & space (Math)—
- Ordering three or more objects by size

MATERIALS

- Blocks or cubes
- Pencil and paper
- Block Tower Graph, p. 87 (one per group)
- Die-cut squares and glue **OR** crayons/ markers

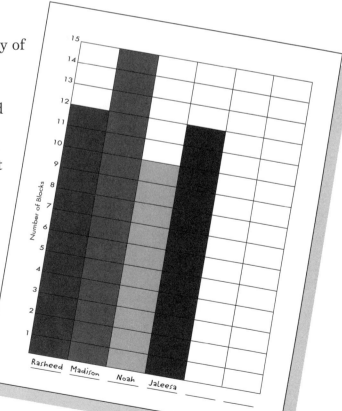

EXTENSIONS

- Have each group work together to try to build the tallest tower.

- Have students estimate how many blocks or cubes the others in their group used, then compare with the actual number.

MODIFICATIONS

- Provide larger blocks for children who have difficulty manipulating the smaller ones.

Students display the bar graphs they made by gluing small colored squares on their papers.

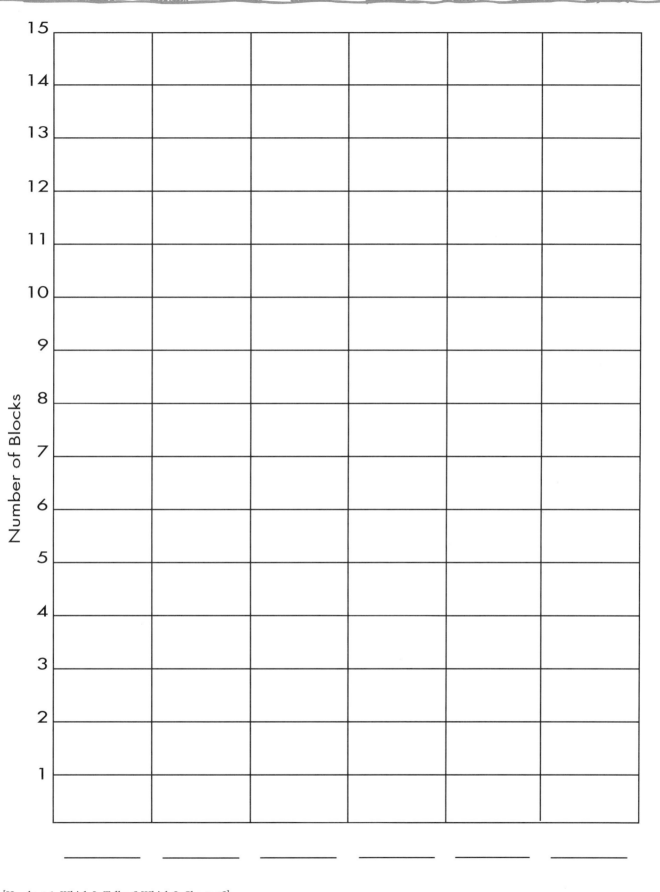

15
14
13
12
11
10
9
8
7
6
5
4
3
2
1

Number of Blocks

_____ _____ _____ _____ _____ _____

[Handout 1: Which Is Tallest? Which Is Shortest?]

WHAT'S LIGHTEST, WHAT'S HEAVIEST?

KEY EXPERIENCES

Measurement of continuous quantity (Math)—

- Ordering objects by weight
- Comparing weights by balance

MATERIALS

- Balance scales
- Various objects from the classroom
- Inch cubes
- "Lightest to Heaviest" handout, p. 90 (one per group)
- Pencil

STORY

Goldilocks and the Three Bears

WORKSHOP SUMMARY

Students weigh a variety of objects in the room, then place them in order by weight. Children complete the activity by following the student instructions.

INSTRUCTIONS

1. Each child chooses two objects from the room to weigh. Objects should be small enough to fit on the scale.

2. The group predicts the order of the objects from lightest to heaviest by looking at the objects. Students write the objects' names in this order on the handout.

3. One child places the first object on the scale and begins to place inch cubes on the other side until the balance is even. The child counts the number of inch cubes needed to balance and writes the number on the handout next to name of the object.

4. Every child in the group should weigh two objects. The group then writes the objects in their actual order on the handout and compares this to initial predictions.

A stapler (in photo at left) weighs a lot more in cubes than a glue stick (at right) does! Students may find that an object is so heavy the counterweight bucket will not hold the necessary number of cubes.

ASSESSMENT

- Compare the groups' final ordering of the objects with the actual measurements.

- Note whether children use comparative words, such as heavier, lighter, heaviest, lightest.

EXTENSIONS

- Have students repeat the workshop using different objects.

- Use another type of scale that accommodates larger or heavier objects.

- Have students choose other manipulatives (besides cubes) to measure the objects.

MODIFICATIONS

- Write the names of the objects for students to copy.

- Choose the objects for children.

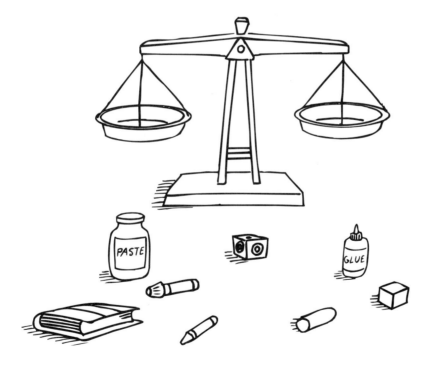

Names _____

LIGHTEST TO HEAVIEST

	Predict order	Weight	Actual order
Lightest	_____	_____	_____
	_____	_____	_____
	_____	_____	_____
	_____	_____	_____
	_____	_____	_____
	_____	_____	_____
	_____	_____	_____
	_____	_____	_____
	_____	_____	_____
	_____	_____	_____
	_____	_____	_____
	_____	_____	_____
	_____	_____	_____
Heaviest	_____	_____	_____

[Handout 1: What's Heaviest, What's Lightest?]

GREAT BIG BEARS, LITTLE TINY BEARS

STORY

Goldilocks and the Three Bears

WORKSHOP SUMMARY

Students arrange teddy bears by size and write comparison statements about the bears. They complete the activity by following the student instructions.

INSTRUCTIONS

1. Children arrange the bears by size, from littlest to biggest. They should use words to compare sizes and to describe position, such as *big, bigger, little/small, littlest/smallest, between, next to,* etc.

2. The children arrange the bears based on the size of another attribute, such as feet, noses, ears, etc.

3. Using the sentence strips as examples or guide words, the children write comparison statements about the bears. For example, *Tayler's is next to DeAndre's; Derek's is bigger than Meghann's; The brown bear comes after the black bear.*

ASSESSMENT

* Check sentences for accuracy and use of positional and comparative words.

* Take anecdotal notes of children as they compare and arrange the bears.

KEY EXPERIENCES

Measurement of continuous quantity (Math)—
* Comparing lengths by side-by-side matching

Geometry & space (Math)—
* Identifying positions and spatial relations

Collections of objects (Math)—
* Ordering members of a set; using "before," "between," "after"

MATERIALS

* Teddy bears or other stuffed animals (students may bring them from home or you may provide)
* Sentence strips with positional words (between, next to, beside, etc.)
* Paper and pencil for each child

EXTENSIONS

- Have children write a story about the group's bears.

- Have students arrange the bears according to one of the other groups' criteria.

MODIFICATIONS

- Provide sentence frames so that students need only insert the identity of each bear, for instance, "_____'s bear is bigger than _____'s bear."

- Assist students as necessary in comparing the bears in different ways using positional and size words.

Haru's bear is bigger than Kate's.

Evan's bear is the smallest.

HIGH TONES, LOW TONES

STORY

Goldilocks and the Three Bears

WORKSHOP SUMMARY

Students experiment with instruments to discover high and low tones. The workshop is teacher-facilitated.

INSTRUCTIONS (TEACHER-FACILITATED)

1. Listen to the song.

2. Discuss the notes heard in the song, naming the lowest and highest ones. Explain that *loudest* and *softest* are not the same as *highest* and *lowest*.

3. Have children explore the instruments to find their lowest and highest tones. Ask students how sounds are made on their instruments.

4. Compare the high and low tones of each instrument. Which instrument has the lowest sound? Which has the highest?

5. Designate an instrument to play along with each of the eight tones in the song (Do, re, mi, fa, so, la, ti, do). For example, the triangle might play when the group sings "Do, a deer, a female deer." The maracas might play when the group sings "Re, a drop of golden sun."

6. Sing the song while playing the instruments.

KEY EXPERIENCES

Exploring instruments (Music)—
- Discovering pitch range

Identifying tone color (Music)—
- Distinguishing the different instrument sounds

Exploring & identifying sounds (Music)—
- Exploring lower/higher and same/different sounds

MATERIALS

- Variety of musical instruments (xylophone, tambourine, triangle, drum, maracas, etc.). If these instruments are not available, use a set of bells or demonstrate on a piano.

- "Do, Re, Mi" music or recording (from *The Sound of Music*)

ASSESSMENT

- Note children's tonal understanding.

- Observe children to see if they can play their instrument on cue.

EXTENSIONS

- Use a set of bells instead of or in addition to the other instruments. Have the group arrange them in order from lowest tone to highest.

- Explore loud and soft sounds with each instrument.

- Provide eight identical jars, a spoon, and a pitcher of water. Have students experiment with different water levels to make various tones. Have them note the pattern and create a scale.

- Have students write down how sounds are made by their instrument.

- Have students explore the size of similar instruments and compare their sounds.

- Ask students to make high and low sounds with their voices. Have them perform the *Goldilocks* story using the appropriately pitched voice for each character (low for Papa Bear, high for Baby Bear, medium for Mama Bear). What do they think Goldilocks would sound like?

MODIFICATIONS

- Adapt instruments as needed for children with motor limitations.

LOST TEETH: MOST TO FEWEST

STORY

How Many Teeth? by Paul Showers

WORKSHOP SUMMARY

Students compare the number of teeth they've lost, make a graph, and answer questions on a questionnaire. This activity is teacher-facilitated.

INSTRUCTIONS (TEACHER-FACILITATED)

1. Read the story to the group.

2. Discuss the number of teeth people have at different stages: baby (0), school age (20), and adult (32).

3. Go over how and why teeth fall out.

4. Ask each student how many teeth he or she has lost. Students can use a mirror to identify any teeth that are growing in.

5. Show the group the bulletin board graph. Explain that it is a picture graph. This means that each student will place a picture—an outline of a tooth—beside the number that indicates how many teeth he or she has lost.

6. Have each student write his or her name on a tooth outline and cut it out (or cut them out ahead of time for students).

7. Have students place their outlines on the appropriate spot on the graph.

KEY EXPERIENCES

Number & numerical operations (Math)—

- Recognizing or counting small sets

Collection of objects (Math)—

- Comparing collections 1-to-1, determining "more," "less," and "same as"

Language, symbols, & graphing (Math)—

- Making picture graphs

MATERIALS

- *How Many Teeth?* by Paul Showers
- Mirrors
- Blank picture graph, prepared on a bulletin board (see example at left)
- Tooth outlines, p. 97 (one per student)
- Teeth Questionnaire, p. 98 (one per student)

8. Referring to the graph, discuss who has lost the fewest teeth and who has lost the most teeth.

9. Have students answer the questions on the questionnaire. Discuss.

ASSESSMENT

• Check questionnaires for accuracy.

EXTENSIONS

• Have students count the number of teeth they have and make a graph.

• Have the group write a poem about teeth.

MODIFICATIONS

• Have students work in pairs to complete the questionnaire.

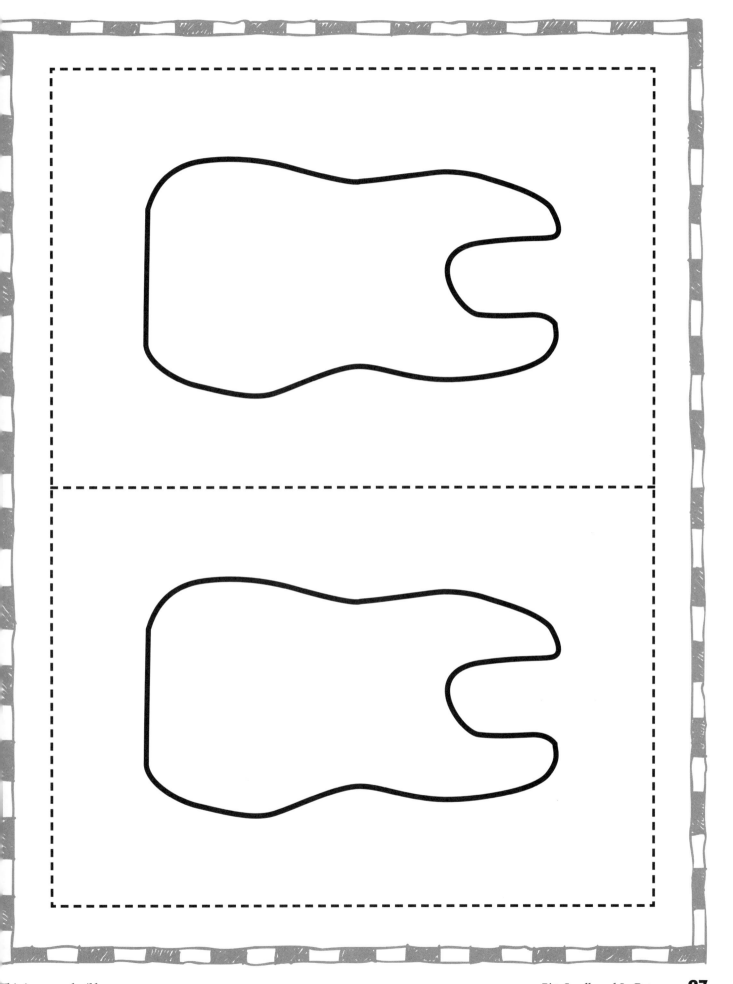

Name _____

TEETH QUESTIONNAIRE

1. How many teeth have you lost?_____

2. How many teeth do you have now?_____

3. What is the least number of teeth lost in your group? _____

4. Who lost the least? _____

5. What is the most number of teeth lost in your group? _____

6. Who lost the most? _____

7. How old were you when you lost your first tooth? _____

8. How old were you when you lost your last tooth? _____

[Handout 1: Lost Teeth: Most to Fewest]

This is a reproducible page.

BIG, SMALL, AND IN BETWEEN RESOURCE LIST

Brett, Jan. (1996). *Goldilocks and the three bears.* New York: PaperStar.

Sammy's science house. [CD-ROM]. Redmond, WA: Edmark.

Showers, Paul. (1991). *How many teeth?* New York: HarperCollins.

12 WAYS TO GET TO 11: A STUDY IN ADDITION

GRADE 1

12 WAYS TO GET TO 11:
A STUDY IN ADDITION
Workshops at a Glance

Note: All the workshops in this section relate to *12 Ways to Get to 11* by Eve Merriam.

Ways to Get to 12 The group works together to find number combinations that add up to 12.	**Picturing Addition** Students write a word problem and draw a picture to go along with it.	**How Many Letters?** Students sort a list of words based on the number of letters in each word.
11 Counters* Students take turns tossing 11 two-color counters and record the number of times different color combinations occur.	**Candy Counting*** The group sorts candies by color and writes a number sentence showing the total number of candies.	**Draw Two** Each student draws two numbered cards from a bag, represents the numbers with different colors of linking cubes, and writes a corresponding number sentence.
Computer Surveys* Each group surveys the class on a different topic and designs symbols on the computer to illustrate the information.	**Apple Addition*** Each student counts the number of seeds in an apple and finds the total number of apple seeds in the group.	**Odd or Even?** The group labels the numbers 1–20 *odd* or *even*.

*Requires direct teacher involvement during all or part of the workshop

The addition workshops in this section are based on the story *12 Ways to Get to 11* by Eve Merriam. This counting book involves a search for the missing number 11. Each two-page spread explores various combinations of items that can be added to reach the number 11. For instance, one illustration shows four banners, five rabbits, a pitcher of water, and a bouquet of flowers in a magician's hat; on another page there is a jack-o'-lantern with two eyes, a nose, and eight teeth.

Each workshop here is designed to increase students' understanding of addition. They will work with a variety of manipulatives to discover that there are many ways to group smaller numbers to equal larger numbers. These hands-on experiences give students a foundation for memorizing addition facts and for adding larger numbers. Several of the workshops involve graphing or other pictorial representations of children's investigations.

Four of the workshops in this section are teacher-facilitated. A whole-group introductory lesson is included that introduces the concept of adding different number combinations to equal a particular sum.

Students use counters and other manipulatives in many of the workshops in this section as they experiment with addends.

$$4 + 7 = 11$$

12 WAYS TO GET TO 11: A STUDY IN ADDITION
Whole-Group Introductory Lesson

MATERIALS

- *12 Ways to Get to 11* by Eve Merriam (one copy per group)
- Paper and pencil for each student
- Linking cubes (11 each of 3 colors per pair of students or small group)

INSTRUCTIONS

Explain that in this activity the class will be exploring the number 11. Read the story *12 Ways to Get to 11,* which presents 12 situations that demonstrate different combinations of objects equaling 11. Divide the class into six groups. If possible, give a copy of the book to each group. If you do not have enough books to go around, type each situation from the book on a sheet of paper ahead of time. Assign each group two of the situations from the book (for example, "Pick up nine pine cones from the forest floor and two acorns"). Have each group write a number sentence that illustrates each assigned situation. For the example of the pine cones and acorns, the group would write $9 + 2 = 11$. If necessary, do an example for the class first. Ask each group to share their situations and number sentences with the whole class. Record each number sentence on the board.

Discuss whether the number combinations students have written are the only ways to add up to 11. Have children pair up or form small groups; give each pair or group three sets of linking cubes, 11 of each color. Ask them to use the cubes to find other ways to get to 11. For example, they might link three red, three blue, and five orange cubes. Each time students find a combination that equals 11, they write down the number sentence that corresponds to that combination. If students have had limited experience with addition, you may choose to give them two colors of cubes rather than three.

After students have had ample opportunity to explore various number combinations with the cubes, as a whole class add the number sentences they

have written to the ones on the board. Have students look over the list carefully to be sure they have not repeated any number sentences. Point out that the same numbers written in a different order are still the same; for example, 9 + 2 = 11 is the same as 2 + 9 = 11. (Illustrate this with the cubes if necessary.) If no one has used 0 and 11 as one combination, discuss this possibility. End the lesson by discussing the total amount of number combinations found and challenging students to look for a pattern to the combinations.

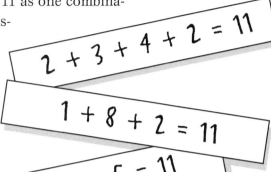

2 + 3 + 4 + 2 = 11

1 + 8 + 2 = 11

4 + 2 + 5 = 11

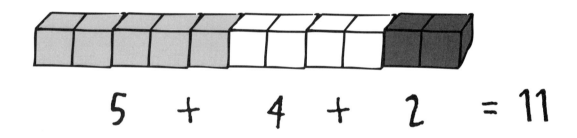

5 + 4 + 2 = 11

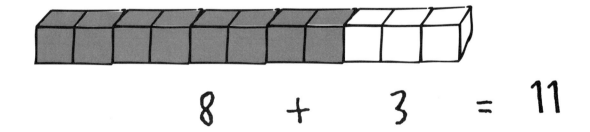

8 + 3 = 11

WAYS TO GET TO 12

STORY

12 Ways to Get to 11

WORKSHOP SUMMARY

Students use manipulatives to find number combinations that add up to 12. This workshop is child-directed; the group can complete it by following the student instructions.

INSTRUCTIONS

1. Each student receives 12 manipulatives, a handout, and a pencil. To help children get started, ask them to recall how they made groups of 11 in the whole-group introductory lesson and what pattern they discovered in their groupings. Challenge students to use their previous discoveries to plan what they will do in this workshop: "How will you group your manipulatives to equal 12? How will you keep track of what you have found? Is there a pattern you will follow?"

2. Students group the manipulatives to come up with as many different combinations as possible that equal 12.

3. As students find the number combinations, they record them on the handout.

4. Compare handouts with the whole group.

KEY EXPERIENCES

Operations on collections of objects (Math)—

- Partitioning a set in various ways; observing the patterns of its subsets

Number & numerical operations (Math)—

- Recognizing addend patterns for a given number

Language, symbols, & graphing (Math)—

- Recognizing and writing numerals and counting words
- Talking about, picturing, and writing about addition and subtraction events; writing number sentences using +, -, and =

MATERIALS

- Math manipulatives in sets of 12
- "Ways to Get to 12" handout, p. 108 (one per student)
- Pencils

ASSESSMENT

- Check that the number sentences are correct. Did students discover several possible combinations?

- Take anecdotal notes as the children answer your questions and as they work. Did they start with a pattern? Did they continue to follow the pattern with all the manipulatives? Did the pattern change as they worked? What kind of verbal reasoning took place during the activity? If students did not describe or follow a pattern as they did the activity, ask them afterwards whether they see a pattern to the number combinations.

EXTENSIONS

- Have each child write and illustrate one of the number sentences. Combine the pages into a book entitled *24 Ways to Count to 12.* (Substitute the number of students in your room for *24.*) The combinations of 12 can be two or three numbers added together.

- Have each group choose another number and explore its addends.

MODIFICATIONS

- Have students explore a smaller number with fewer addends.

- Have students pair up.

- Provide one-on-one instruction if necessary.

Pages from a class-made book show students' understanding of grouping numbers together as addends for 11.

Name _____

WAYS TO GET TO 12

	First Number	+	Second Number	=	12
1.	_____	+	_____	=	_____
2.	_____	+	_____	=	_____
3.	_____	+	_____	=	_____
4.	_____	+	_____	=	_____
5.	_____	+	_____	=	_____
6.	_____	+	_____	=	_____
7.	_____	+	_____	=	_____
8.	_____	+	_____	=	_____
9.	_____	+	_____	=	_____
10.	_____	+	_____	=	_____

[Handout 1: Ways to Get to 12]

This is a reproducible page.

PICTURING ADDITION

STORY

12 Ways to Get to 11

WORKSHOP SUMMARY

Following the pattern of *12 Ways to Get to 11,* students make a design or picture and write a number sentence and word problem about it. The workshop is child-directed; the group completes the activity by following the student instructions.

INSTRUCTIONS

1. Students look at the themes and illustrations in the story to get ideas for their own illustrations and corresponding number sentences.

2. Each member of the group chooses a different theme to illustrate, such as food, animals, or sports. Before they begin drawing, students write the number sentence they are going to illustrate (for example, *4 + 6 = 10).* You may want to limit the number of objects illustrated by having students write only number sentences that equal 12 or less. To help students get started, ask them what number sentence they are going to use and how they will show the numbers in their picture.

3. Once students have completed their drawing, they write the word problem that describes their picture and corresponds to their number sentence. (For example, *4 blueberries and 6 strawberries equal 10 berries.)* Ask students what statement they are going to write to describe their picture.

KEY EXPERIENCES

Language, symbols, & graphing (Math)—

- Talking about, picturing, and writing about addition and subtraction events; writing number sentences using +, -, and =

- Drawing and tracing shapes

MATERIALS

- *12 Ways to Get to 11* by Eve Merriam
- Pencil
- Crayons or markers
- Construction paper

$$4 \text{ blueberries} + 6 \text{ strawberries} = 10 \text{ berries}$$

ASSESSMENT

- Check whether students' number sentences and word problems match their illustrations.

- Look for creativity in the themes and illustrations.

EXTENSIONS

- Have students write the word problem on the back of their paper rather than the front, then trade pictures with one another and figure out the new word problem.

- Bind the illustrations into a class book.

MODIFICATIONS

- Have students choose a prewritten number sentence to illustrate.

- Model/facilitate the process the first day and have students complete the workshop independently the second.

- Have older students write out the word problems for younger students who need assistance (or write them out yourself).

- Provide magazine pictures for children.

HOW MANY LETTERS?

STORY

12 Ways to Get to 11

WORKSHOP SUMMARY

Students sort a list of words from the story based on the number of letters in the words. This activity is child-directed; the group can complete the workshop by following the student instructions.

INSTRUCTIONS

1. Students count the number of letters in each of the words on the word list.

2. Either individually (on separate charts) or as a group, students write the words in the corresponding columns on the number chart.

ASSESSMENT

- Check for accuracy in counting. Could students always tell by looking at the words which had more or fewer letters? (For instance, *triplets* and *piglets* look the same length, but *triplets* actually has more letters; *banners* looks longer then *rabbits,* but they both have seven letters.)

- Observe the groups' cooperation. How do they decide to do the activity—do they divide up the words and assign some to each person, do some members count while others write, or do they find some other method?

KEY EXPERIENCES

Number & numerical operations (Math)—
- Using the words "one, two, three, ..." in consistent order when attempting to count beyond small sets

Collections of objects (Math)—
- Sorting a collection, then re-sorting with new criteria

MATERIALS
- Word List (p. 113)
- "How Many Letters?" handout, pp. 114–115 (one per student *or* per group)
- Pencil

eyes
pond
boat
flag

flowers
popcorn
rabbits
bouquet
traffic

EXTENSIONS

- Have students write summary statements on the back of their charts, explaining how many words had each number of letters, which words had the most or fewest letters, etc.

- Repeat the activity with spelling words, words around the room, or words in a different story. Compare these lists with the word list.

- Place student names (or have students write their own) on a new chart and have them compare lengths.

MODIFICATIONS

- If necessary, spread this activity over two or more workshop periods—or give students only half the words at a time.

- Cut the words out and have children glue them in the appropriate columns on the chart. Or, write them on index cards and have students place the cards on a poster-sized version of the chart.

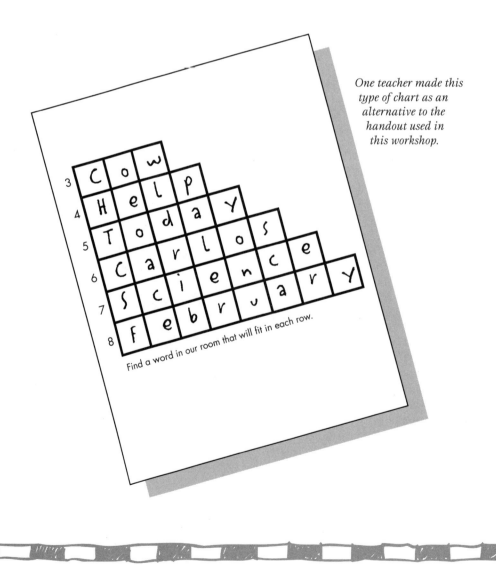

One teacher made this type of chart as an alternative to the handout used in this workshop.

WORD LIST

traffic	lights	flowers	twins
forest	garage	cars	bicycle
acorns	bites	core	stem
circus	seeds	boat	masts
peanut	soil	preservers	flag
shells	ladder	anchor	turtles
popcorn	frogs	catalog	dragonflies
magician	pond	jack-o-lantern	teeth
banners	eyes	nose	mailbox
rabbits	letters	packages	corners
pitcher	postcard	triplets	chimneys
water	sow	piglets	hen
bouquet	eggs	beaks	

[Handout 1: How Many Letters?]

Name _____

HOW MANY LETTERS?

3	4	5	6	7

[Handout 2: How Many Letters?]

This is a reproducible page.

8	9	10	11	12

11 COUNTERS

STORY

12 Ways to Get to 11

WORKSHOP SUMMARY

Students take turns tossing 11 two-color counters and record the resulting number sentences. This activity is teacher-facilitated.

INSTRUCTIONS (TEACHER-FACILITATED)

1. Work with the group to list the combinations of numbers that add up to 11 ($1 + 10, 2 + 9, 3 + 8, 4 + 7, 5 + 6$). (You may refer to the chart developed during the whole-group introductory lesson.) Have them fill in the top of each column of the Counter Toss chart with one of these combinations, discussing why $6 + 5 = 5 + 6$ and why it is not necessary to have separate columns for these addend pairs.

2. Have each child take a turn tossing the counters.

3. Have children then color in a box in the appropriate column of their chart. The game ends when one column is filled.

   This game actually demonstrates probability. Children will notice that some combinations of numbers occur more often than others when they toss the counters. Discuss probability and encourage children to play again to see if they get similar results.

ASSESSMENT

* Observe the children as they play the game, noting any comments they make about patterns or the frequency of a set of numbers tossed.

KEY EXPERIENCES

Operations on collections of objects (Math)—

* Partitioning a set in various ways; observing the pattern of its subsets

Numbers & numerical operations (Math)—

* Using the words "one, two, three, ..." in consistent order when attempting to count beyond small sets
* Using one word for each item counted, when counting beyond small sets
* Recognizing addend patterns for a given number

MATERIALS

* Cup
* 11 two-color counters (red on one side, yellow on the other)
* Counter Toss chart, p. 118 (one per child)
* Colored pencils

$$4 + 7 = 11$$

EXTENSIONS

- Play again to see if the same combination of numbers wins. Discuss children's observations.

- Play the game using the number 12.

- Add *probability* to the class vocabulary/spelling list.

MODIFICATIONS

- Write the number combinations at the top or bottom of the chart ahead of time.

In this workshop children discover that some number combinations occur more frequently than others. Encourage them to explore the reason for this.

Name _____

COUNTER TOSS

[Handout 1: 11 Counters]

CANDY COUNTING

STORY

12 Ways to Get to 11

WORKSHOP SUMMARY

Students sort multicolored candies and write a number sentence representing the total number of candies. This activity is teacher-facilitated.

INSTRUCTIONS (TEACHER-FACILITATED)

1. Give each group a bag of candy or a baggie with a specific number of candies in it.

2. Ask students to sort the candy by color.

3. When all the candy is sorted, each member of the group chooses a pile (of one color) to draw a representation of. Students should use the corresponding color of crayon and draw on separate pieces of paper.

4. Underneath their illustration, students write the total number of candies on their page.

5. On a separate piece of paper, the group writes a number sentence showing the amount of candy of each color and the total number of candies.

6. Encourage students to figure out a way to evenly distribute the candy to be eaten.

This group sorted Smarties candies by color and added the total number of candies.

KEY EXPERIENCES

Collections of objects (Math)—

- Sorting objects into many small groups based on common attributes

Language, symbols, & graphing (Math)—

- Talking about, picturing, and writing about addition and subtraction events; writing number sentences using +, -, and =

MATERIALS

- Multicolored candies (Skittles, M&M's, etc.) or different-colored nonedible objects if you prefer (blocks, manipulatives)
- Crayons that match the candy colors
- Paper (one sheet per child)
- Pencil

ASSESSMENT

- Check the accuracy of each group's number sentence.

EXTENSIONS

- Repeat with another bag of the same candy to see if the total amount and color distribution are the same. Or, have groups compare their results with one another's.

- Repeat with a different type of candy or manipulative.

- Assist students in writing summary sentences comparing the amount of each color—for example, *There are more red than blue M&M's. There are 13 yellow and 10 orange. 13 > 10.* Or, make a worksheet for students to fill in with this information.

- Have students sort the candy or manipulatives based on another criteria.

- Have the students pair up to write and draw number sentences for their two colors. They each then find a new partner and repeat.

MODIFICATIONS

- Have students do this workshop individually or in pairs rather than as a group.

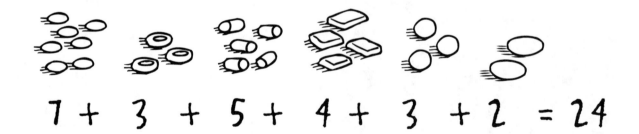

$$7 + 3 + 5 + 4 + 3 + 2 = 24$$

DRAW TWO

STORY

12 Ways to Get to 11

WORKSHOP SUMMARY

Each student draws two number cards from a bag, represents them with different colors of linking cubes, and writes a corresponding number sentence. This workshop is child-directed; the group can complete it by following the student instructions.

INSTRUCTIONS

1. Each student draws two number cards from the paper bag.

2. The child links cubes together to represent each number shown on the cards, using two different colors of cubes.

3. On the grid paper, the student colors in the same number of sections as linking cubes.

4. The child can either cut out the representation on the grid paper, glue it to another piece of paper, and write the corresponding number sentence beside it; or he or she can write the number sentence on the grid paper beside the representation.

5. Children may repeat the process with a new set of numbers as time allows.

KEY EXPERIENCES

Language, symbols, & graphing (Math)—

- Recognizing and writing numerals and counting words

- Talking about, picturing, and writing about addition and subtraction events; writing number sentences using +, -, and =

MATERIALS

- Number cards labeled 0–11, p. 123 (2 sets per group)
- Small paper bag
- Linking cubes of various colors
- Grid paper
- Crayons or markers
- Paper and pencil
- Scissors
- Glue or tape

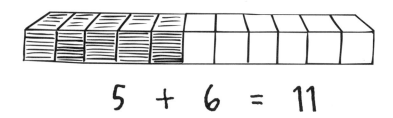

$$5 + 6 = 11$$

ASSESSMENT

- Check that the number sentences are correct.

- Take anecdotal notes as children work with the materials. Were they able to match the number of cubes with the numerals? How many did each child complete?

EXTENSIONS

- Have students roll two dice instead of using number cards.

- Make number cards labeled 11–20 and have students repeat the workshop.

MODIFICATIONS

- Have students work with a partner.

0	1	2
3	4	5
6	7	8
9	10	11

COMPUTER SURVEYS

STORY

12 Ways to Get to 11

WORKSHOP SUMMARY

Each group surveys the class on a different topic and designs symbols on the computer to illustrate the information. More than one workshop period may be needed to complete this teacher-facilitated activity.

INSTRUCTIONS (TEACHER-FACILITATED)

1. Each group chooses a different topic on which to survey the class; for example, favorite candy, fruit, drink, or restaurant, or least favorite vegetable. Groups should brainstorm ahead of time so that each group picks a different topic and so there is enough time to conduct the survey.

2. Students narrow their topic to five choices. For example, the choices of favorite drinks could be milk, water, soft drink, juice, and tea.

3. Each member of the group makes a chart like the following:

Favorite Drink
milk
water
soft drink
juice
tea

4. Each student takes a chart to another group and asks each member to choose one of the items listed. The surveyor then makes a tally beside each child's choice.

5. The group members take their charts back to the workshop area and combine their information into one master chart. (Remind them to survey themselves.)

6. Using the master chart, students design an illustration on the computer to show the survey information. Each student could illustrate a different survey choice. For example, one child might draw nine cows to depict the number of children who chose milk as their favorite drink.

KEY EXPERIENCES

Language, symbols, & graphing (Math)—

- Making pictures and diagrams showing 1-to-1 correspondence
- Talking about, picturing, and writing about addition events; writing number sentences using +, -, =
- Using words, pictures, and models to represent experiences with counting

MATERIALS

- Computers/printers
- Computer program: *Kid Pix Deluxe* (Broderbund Software)
- Paper
- Pencils

7. At the bottom of the illustration, the child types in the numeral corresponding to the number of objects pictured.

8. Students print and post their survey results.

ASSESSMENT

*   Evaluate whether children depicted the appropriate number of children for their part of the topic.

*   Ask students to summarize, either orally or on paper, their results. For example, *13 children like soda, 5 like milk, and 7 like juice; More kids like milk than water;* or *Juice is the class's favorite drink.*

EXTENSIONS

*   Have students give an oral presentation regarding their survey findings.

*   Have students design a blind taste test. Students taste each choice of food or drink without seeing it and choose their favorite.

MODIFICATIONS

*   Pair children to work on the computer.

*   Make a blank survey chart ahead of time; children can fill in the information they will be collecting.

*   If computers or appropriate software are not available, have students illustrate their survey results by hand.

What vegetable is your least favorite?

What TV shows do you like best?

What's your favorite drink?

APPLE ADDITION

STORY

12 Ways to Get to 11

WORKSHOP SUMMARY

Each student counts the number of seeds in an apple and finds the total number of seeds of all the apples in the group. This workshop is teacher-facilitated.

INSTRUCTIONS (TEACHER-FACILITATED)

1. Give each child in the group an apple.

2. Ask the children to predict how many seeds they think are in the apples.

3. Cut the apples in half or quarters and have children remove the seeds.

4. Have each child count the seeds in his or her apple and write the number on one side of the apple-shaped paper. Then have children draw the number of seeds on the back of their paper.

5. Lay the apple pages side by side, with the numerals face up. Ask the children to come up with a number sentence that adds all of the seeds together. Write this on the back of the sentence strip.

6. Ask students to make up a word problem about the number of seeds in the group's apples. Have them write the word problem on the front of the sentence strip. (For example, *Tommy had 2 seeds, Dewayne had 4, and Juanita had 3. How many seeds did we have?*)

7. Hang the paper apples seed-side up in the math area. Place the sentence strip beneath the apples.

8. Have groups solve one another's word problems. Children can check their answers by looking at the number sentence on the back of the sentence strip.

KEY EXPERIENCES

Number & numerical operations (Math)—

- Using one word for each item counted, when counting beyond small sets

Language, symbols, & graphing (Math)—

- Recognizing and writing numerals and counting words

- Talking about, picturing, and writing about addition and subtraction events; writing number sentences using +, -, and =

MATERIALS

- Apples (one per child)
- Knife
- Paper towels
- Apple-shaped construction paper (one per child)
- Pencils (one per child)
- Marker
- Sentence strips (one per group)

ASSESSMENT

- Take anecdotal notes on how children participate in the process of counting the apple seeds, writing the corresponding number, and adding all the seeds together.

EXTENSIONS

- Use small pumpkins (and pumpkin-shaped paper) instead of apples.

- Give each group a different fruit or vegetable.

MODIFICATIONS

- Have students glue the seeds instead of draw them.

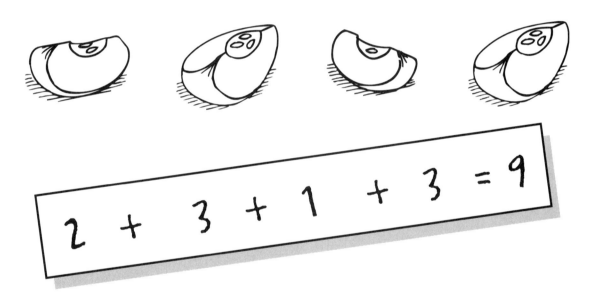

ODD OR EVEN?

STORY

12 Ways to Get to 11

WORKSHOP SUMMARY

Groups explore the numbers 1–20 to determine if they are odd or even. This workshop is child-directed; the group can complete it by following the student instructions after a teacher-led mini-lesson.

INSTRUCTIONS

Mini-lesson:

Discuss the concepts of *odd* and *even* with the class. You may want to use the number 11 to keep with the theme of this group of workshops. Count out 11 manipulatives, then separate them, one by one, into two piles, explaining that you want to have the same number in each pile. They will observe that you have one left over. Explain that if you have one left over when you separate a certain number into two equal piles, that number is considered odd *(odd* means something doesn't fit or is left over). If there is not one left over and the number of objects can be equally split into two piles, then the number is even. Ask the class whether the number 11 is odd or even.

Workshop:

1. Working in pairs and using manipulatives, children repeat the mini-lesson procedure for numbers 1–20. Next to each number on the handout, they write *even* or *odd,* based on their experimentations with the manipulatives. (Students may write *odd* next to 11 based on what they observed in the mini-lesson.)

2. Students solve the bonus problem at the bottom of the handout.

The concepts of odd and even become more concrete when children divide manipulatives into two groups and observe whether the number of objects divides evenly or there is one left over.

KEY EXPERIENCE

Collections of objects (Math)—

• Comparing collections 1-to-1 to determine "more," "less," and "the same as"

MATERIALS

• Math manipulatives
• "Odd or Even" handout, p. 130 (one per pair of students)
• Pencils

ASSESSMENT

- Check students' papers for accuracy.

- Ask questions to check students' understanding, such as "Is *2* an even or odd number? How do you know?"

EXTENSIONS

- On the back of the handout, ask children to write two to three statements about any patterns they observe. For example, *They go odd, even, odd, even; The numbers with 2s are even.*

- Have students write the numbers 1–10 in one column of their paper and 11–20 in another column, lining up the two columns across from each other. Do they notice a pattern of odd and even numbers? (Numbers that end in the same numeral—2 and 12, 5 and 15—are both either even or odd.)

- If children are able to count by 2s, have them look for another pattern with the numbers 2, 4, 6, 8, and so on. (They are all even.)

- Have students repeat the workshop with the numbers 21–40.

MODIFICATIONS

- Have children dictate their observations.

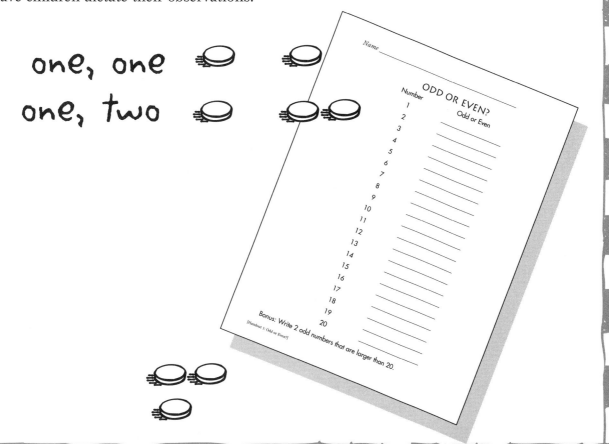

ODD OR EVEN?

Number	Odd or Even
1	_____
2	_____
3	_____
4	_____
5	_____
6	_____
7	_____
8	_____
9	_____
10	_____
11	_____
12	_____
13	_____
14	_____
15	_____
16	_____
17	_____
18	_____
19	_____
20	_____

Bonus: Write 2 odd numbers that are larger than 20.

[Handout 1: Odd or Even?]

A STUDY IN ADDITION RESOURCE LIST

Baker, Keith. (1999). *Quack and count.* San Diego: Harcourt Brace.

Kid Pix Deluxe [CD-ROM]. Novato, CA: Broderbund Software.

Merriam, Eve. (1996). *12 ways to get to 11.* New York: Aladdin Paperbacks.

TEN PENNIES
FOR A DIME

GRADE 2

TEN PENNIES FOR A DIME
Workshops at a Glance

Anthony and Nicholas*	**$1.00 Words**	**Combinations of $1.00***
Students calculate how much money Anthony and Nicholas, Alexander's brothers, had. *Alexander, Who Used to Be Rich Last Sunday.*	Students find the monetary value of their spelling words. *Alexander, Who Used to Be Rich Last Sunday.*	Students find as many combinations of coins as possible that equal $1.00. *Alexander, Who Used to Be Rich Last Sunday.*
Draw a Penny	**How Much Water Can a Penny Hold?**	**Penny Art**
Students draw a penny from memory, then observe one for a minute, add what they have left off, then look at the penny again and add final touches. *Benny's Pennies.*	Students investigate surface tension as they place drops of water on a penny. *Benny's Pennies.*	Students make a drawing or design by tracing a penny. *Benny's Pennies.*
Money in a Jar*	**How Much Money?***	**Milk Money**
Students sort and count money in a jar. *A Chair for My Mother.*	Students use money manipulatives to add up all the money the Pigs found. *Pigs Will Be Pigs.*	Students figure the cost of the class's milk for a day if everyone bought it. *Anabelle Swift, Kindergartner.*

Requires direct teacher involvement during all or part of the workshop

The intriguing but often confusing concept of money is the focus of the workshops in this section. The five books used here present this concept in meaningful contexts to help children see how money relates to their everyday lives.

Children are introduced to the workshops through Judith Viorst's *Alexander, Who Used to Be Rich Last Sunday.* Alexander, who along with his brothers receives a dollar from his grandparents when they come to visit, finds himself in a few days with only a few junk items and some bus tokens. The story takes readers through Alexander's misadventures with his money. Unlike Alexander, Benny *(Benny's Pennies,* Pat Brisson) receives only five pennies to spend, but with suggestions from his family and the generosity of neighbors and friends, he is able to spend his money wisely and unselfishly. The emphasis in *A Chair for My Mother* (Vera B. Williams) is on saving money—for a special chair for Rosa's mother to replace the one lost in their house fire. Rosa, her mother, and her grandmother contribute what they can to the saving jar until it is full and they can all start shopping for their special chair. The Pig family in *Pigs Will Be Pigs* (Amy Axelrod) didn't have the foresight to save money or go to the bank and find themselves short on cash for dinner. They are able to afford a special meal at their favorite restaurant by going on a money hunt around the house. At the end of the book children are encouraged to add up the amount of money the Pigs found, how much they spent on dinner, and how much they had left over. Thanks to the inclusion of the restaurant menu, readers can also put together different orders using the amount of money the Pigs had. Counting is something Annabelle Swift, Kindergartner (in the book by the same title, written by Amy Schwartz), has learned how to do before entering kindergarten, thanks to her big sister. Annabelle amazes everyone on the first day of school when she counts up the class's milk money.

As they participate in these workshops, students will gain a variety of experiences in counting money and making exchanges among equivalent amounts. Most of the activities use money manipulatives. Students will also explore some of the physical properties of coins as they investigate the features with a magnifying glass, use tracings to make designs, and experiment with surface tension. Several of the workshops involve the use of calculators; if your students do not have prior experience with calculators, you may want to provide some time to explore them before beginning those workshops.

TEN PENNIES FOR A DIME
Whole-Group Introductory Lesson

MATERIALS

- Two jars of money—one with $7 in quarters, the other with $6 in nickels and dimes
- *Alexander, Who Used to Be Rich Last Sunday* by Judith Viorst
- Chart paper and/or overhead projector, marker

INSTRUCTIONS

Show the class the two jars of money. Ask which jar students would rather have, the jar with quarters or the one with nickels and dimes. They are likely to indicate the one with nickels and dimes, because it has more coins.

Ask the class how much money a nickel, dime, and quarter are each worth. Now ask them to look at the jars again and choose which one they would rather have. Together count the quarters, then ask how many quarters equal a dollar. Tell the class the total of the quarters. Repeat for the nickels and dimes. Compare the amounts of the quarters and the nickels and dimes.

Read *Alexander, Who Used to Be Rich Last Sunday.* Discuss whether Alexander spent his money wisely or not. Ask the children if $1.00 really is a lot of money. Reread the story, this time using the overhead or chart paper to subtract the amounts Alexander spent and lost.

Finally, have each child finish the sentence, "If I had $1.00 ..." Share the children's ideas by recording them on chart paper.

Quarters

Nickles and Dimes

ANTHONY AND NICHOLAS

STORY

Alexander, Who Used to Be Rich Last Sunday by Judith Viorst

WORKSHOP SUMMARY

Students calculate how much money Anthony and Nicholas, Alexander's brothers, had. This workshop is teacher-facilitated.

INSTRUCTIONS (TEACHER-FACILITATED)

1. The group turns to the first page of the book. Students read how many coins and bills Anthony had and place the same amount of money manipulatives in front of themselves. They should place their money in the same order as Anthony's is listed—from greatest to least value.

2. Starting with the coins of the least value, students exchange them for equivalent coins or bills. To assist, ask such questions as "What can you exchange for the 18 pennies?" Help them see that they could exchange 10 of the pennies for a dime and 5 of the remaining 8 pennies for a nickel.

3. Once all exchanges have been made, students add the money, beginning with the bills. They write the total amount on their paper.

4. Students repeat the process to total Nicholas's money. Who had more?

ASSESSMENT

• Take anecdotal notes as children exchange the money and add the amounts.

EXTENSIONS

• Ask children to total the amount of money the two brothers had at the beginning of the story.

• Provide other storybooks with money problems for students to solve.

MODIFICATIONS

• Provide individual assistance for children as necessary.

KEY EXPERIENCES

Language, symbols, and graphing (Math)—

• Talking about, picturing, and writing about addition and subtraction events

Number & numerical operations (Math)—

• Grouping and regrouping objects to correspond to addition and subtraction of multi-digit numbers

• Making exchanges between equivalent sets of coins

MATERIALS

• *Alexander, Who Used to Be Rich Last Sunday* by Judith Viorst

• Money manipulatives

• Paper

• Pencil

$1.00 WORDS

STORY

Alexander, Who Used to Be Rich Last Sunday

WORKSHOP SUMMARY

Students find the monetary value of their spelling words. This workshop is child-directed and can be completed by following the student instructions.

INSTRUCTIONS

1. Each student writes the first spelling word vertically on his or her paper.

2. Beside each letter, students write its monetary value based on the Alphabet List handout.

3. By hand or using a calculator, students add up the word's amounts.

4. Students compare answers with one another. If someone's answer does not match the rest of the group's, students work together to find the error.

5. Students repeat the process until they have found the value of the rest of the words.

ASSESSMENT

- Check for accuracy in addition.

EXTENSIONS

- Ask students to identify the least expensive and most expensive words on the list. Do any equal $1.00 exactly?

- Challenge students to think of words that equal $1.00.

- Have students make a graph of the monetary value of their spelling words.

- Have students add up the value of their names or of words from the story.

KEY EXPERIENCES

Writing (Language & literacy)—

- Acquiring, strengthening, and extending writing skills: Spelling

Language, symbols, & graphing (Math)—

- Writing number sentences using +, -, =
- Writing multi-digit numbers

MATERIALS

- Alphabet List, p. 140 (one per group)
- List of class spelling words (one per group)
- Paper and pencil for each student
- Calculators

M	.13
O	.15
N	.14
E	.05
Y	.25
	.72

MODIFICATIONS

- Provide grid paper to help children line up the numbers to add.

- Before the workshop, do some examples of the activity using students' names.

BACKGROUND READING

The $1.00 Word Riddle Book, by Marilyn Burns, 1993, New York: Addison Wesley Longman.

ALPHABET LIST

A	=	.01	N =	.14
B	=	.02	O =	.15
C	=	.03	P =	.16
D	=	.04	Q =	.17
E	=	.05	R =	.18
F	=	.06	S =	.19
G	=	.07	T =	.20
H	=	.08	U =	.21
I	=	.09	V =	.22
J	=	.10	W =	.23
K	=	.11	X =	.24
L	=	.12	Y =	.25
M	=	.13	Z =	.26

[Handout 1: $1.00 words]

This is a reproducible page.

COMBINATIONS OF $1.00

STORY

Alexander, Who Used to Be Rich Last Sunday

WORKSHOP SUMMARY

Students find as many combinations of coins as possible that equal $1.00. This activity is teacher-facilitated.

KEY EXPERIENCES

Language, symbols, & graphing (Math)—

- Using words, pictures, and models to represent experiences with counting

Number & numerical operations (Math)—

- Making exchanges between equivalent sets of coins

INSTRUCTIONS

1. The group works together to find as many combinations of coins that equal $1.00 as possible. Students can begin with four quarters and exchange them, one at a time, for equivalent coins. If necessary, limit the number of combinations children are expected to find.

2. The group can choose how to display their findings—by making a written list or a drawing of the different combinations of coins.

ASSESSMENT

- Assess the groups' lists for accuracy.

EXTENSIONS

- Combine all of the groups' lists into one, showing all of the different combinations found.

- Have students write about what they would do with $1.00, or $100.

- Have students write about how much money they would like to get from their grandparents (or someone else) and how they would spend it.

- Instead of $1.00, give students another amount for which to find combinations of coins.

MATERIALS

- Money manipulatives or actual money

- Paper and pencil for each group

MODIFICATIONS

- Provide coin stickers for children to use.

- Provide a picture key showing coin equivalents, for instance, five pennies equal a nickel.

KEY EXPERIENCES

Observing (Science)—

- Looking at familiar things in a new way: Observing closely, systematically, and objectively

Language, symbols, & graphing (Math)—

- Making pictures and diagrams showing 1-to-1 correspondence

MATERIALS

- *Benny's Pennies* by Pat Brisson
- Pennies (one per child)
- Magnifying glasses (one per child)
- Paper and pencil for each child
- Timer

DRAW A PENNY

STORY

Benny's Pennies by Pat Brisson

WORKSHOP SUMMARY

Students draw a penny without looking at one, then observe one for one minute, add what they have left off, then look at the penny again and add final touches. This workshop is child-directed and can be completed by following the student instructions.

INSTRUCTIONS

1. The group reads the story together.

2. Each member of the group draws a picture of a penny's head and tail without looking at a penny. Encourage them to draw the penny large enough for them to include all the details. They should spend about two minutes.

3. When everyone is ready, one child sets the timer for one minute. During the minute, the children look at the penny closely using the magnifying glass.

4. After the minute is up, they return to their drawing and add details they forgot the first time.

5. When they have added all they can remember, they compare the penny to their drawing and add any missing elements.

ASSESSMENT

- Note how students observe the penny and how much detail they are able to remember. Do they notice new features each time they observe?

EXTENSIONS

- Challenge students to guess how many pennies can fit on a piece of paper (in a single layer). Have them try it and record the actual number.

- Have students compare what is on a penny to what is on other coins.

- Have students find equivalent coins for varying amounts of pennies.

- Ask students to create a new coin. They should design it, name it, tell how much it is worth, and explain why it would be useful.

- Bring in, or ask students to bring in, coins from other countries and compare them to U.S. coins. Share information about where the foreign coins are used, what they are called, how much they are worth, and what the writing on them says.

MODIFICATIONS

- Have students work with a peer to complete the drawing.

HOW MUCH WATER CAN A PENNY HOLD?

STORY

Benny's Pennies

WORKSHOP SUMMARY

Students investigate surface tension as they place drops of water on a penny. This activity is child-directed and can be completed by following the student instructions.

INSTRUCTIONS

1. Each student receives a penny, paper towel, eyedropper, and a cup of water.

2. Students put the penny on the paper towel and place themselves at eye level with it.

3. Slowly, one drop at a time, they add water to the penny with the eyedropper, counting each drop.

4. Each student records on the sheet of paper the number of drops the penny holds before the water overflows.

5. Students dry their penny and perform the experiment again in an attempt to put even more drops on it.

6. Each person records the highest number of drops achieved.

ASSESSMENT

- Take anecdotal notes while children count their drops.

- In a whole-class discussion of the activity, ask the children about their observations and what they think kept the water on the penny for so long. Discuss cohesion (surface tension) with them, which is a property of liquids that gives the surface a slightly elastic quality and enables the liquid to form separate drops. Water molecules are pulled in by the surface tension, which helps hold the water on the penny.

KEY EXPERIENCES

Reporting & interpreting data & results (Science)—

- Discussing observations

Observing, predicting, & controlling change (Science)—

- Manipulating physical objects to produce an effect or change

Number & numerical operations (Math)—

- Using one word for each item counted

MATERIALS

- Pennies (one per student)
- Water
- Eyedroppers
- Paper towels
- Cups
- Paper and pencil

EXTENSIONS

- Have students do the experiment on both sides of the penny and compare the two amounts.

- Have students try the experiment with soapy water. What do they notice?

- Have students use a nickel, dime, or quarter and predict which will hold the most water. Have them compare the number of drops on these coins with those held by a penny.

- Provide books for children to learn more about the subject of surface tension.

MODIFICATIONS

- Provide a baster for children who have difficulty manipulating the eyedropper.

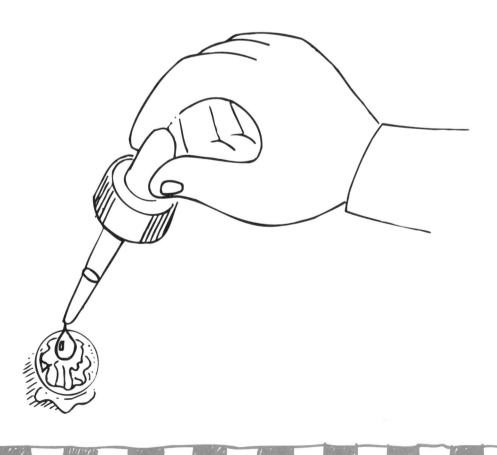

PENNY ART

KEY EXPERIENCES

Language, symbols, & graphing (Math)—
- Drawing and tracing shapes

MATERIALS
- Pennies
- Pencils, markers, crayons, map pencils, and other art materials
- Paper of various types and colors

STORY

Benny's Pennies

WORKSHOP SUMMARY

Students make a drawing or design by tracing a penny. This workshop is child-directed and can be completed by following the student instructions.

INSTRUCTIONS

1. Each student chooses a type and color of paper to work with.

2. Students trace a penny on the paper. They can make a drawing or design by tracing the penny several times on the paper, or they can trace and cut out several pennies and glue them on another piece of paper in a design.

3. Students choose from a variety of art materials to complete their designs.

ASSESSMENT

- Look for accuracy in drawing, tracing, and cutting out shapes, as well as creativity.

EXTENSIONS

- Have children title their artwork and write a short description of it.
- Have children count the number of pennies they used.

MODIFICATIONS

- Provide precut penny shapes for children who may have difficulty tracing and cutting the small shapes.

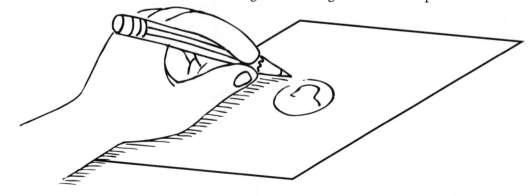

MONEY IN A JAR

STORY

A Chair for My Mother by Vera B. Williams

WORKSHOP SUMMARY

Students sort and count money in a jar. This activity is teacher-facilitated to assist children with counting the money.

INSTRUCTIONS (TEACHER-FACILITATED)

1. Read the story with the group.

2. Discuss saving money. Talk about the change this family saved—why they saved it, how long students think it took them to save, how much change they think it would have taken, etc.

3. Place the jar of money in front of the group. Explain that the group is going to sort the change. Ask "How much money do you think is in the jar?" Write down children's answers. Ask them what they think would be the easiest way to count the money.

4. Have students sort the change by pennies, nickels, dimes, and quarters. Ask students to think of a way to group each kind of coin to make it easier to count them—for instance, putting quarters in groups of 4, dimes in groups of 10, nickels in groups of 20. How could they group the pennies?

5. Give each student (or pair of students) a pile of change to sort based on their discussion.

6. Counting one type of change at a time, together add up the money to see how much was in the jar. Write down the amount, along with the number of coins of each type.

7. Discuss whose predictions were closest.

KEY EXPERIENCES

Collections of objects (Math)—

- Sorting a collection, then re-sorting with new criteria
- Grouping and counting objects by 2s, 5s, 10s

Language, symbols, & graphing (Math)—

- Talking about, picturing, and writing about addition and subtraction events

MATERIALS

- Small jar filled with variety of change (play or real)
- *A Chair for My Mother* by Vera B. Williams
- Paper
- Pencil

Teacher facilitation is helpful as students group coins and add up their value.

ASSESSMENT

- Check for understanding of how many coins of each type equal a dollar.
- Take anecdotal notes as children sort and count the money. How do they decide to group each type of coin?

EXTENSIONS

- Ask students to make a list of things the class could do with the money.
- Have students weigh each type of coin to see which weighs the most.
- Have students collect money for a charity or for an item for the classroom.
- Provide a commercial board game in which students exchange money.
- Ask students to write about something they and their family would save for and how they would earn the money.

MODIFICATIONS

- Provide assistance with sorting and counting as needed.

HOW MUCH MONEY?

STORY

Pigs Will Be Pigs by Amy Axelrod

WORKSHOP SUMMARY

Students use money manipulatives to add up all the money the Pigs found. This activity is teacher-facilitated to assist students with counting money.

INSTRUCTIONS (TEACHER-FACILITATED)

1. Read the story together. List all the places the Pigs looked for money.

2. Reread the story, with the group using money manipulatives to represent how much money the Pigs have located. Stop after each amount found to allow children to count out the correct amounts.

3. At the end have children total their money, exchanging for larger coins or bills if necessary. Check the group's answer by comparing with the story's.

KEY EXPERIENCES

Reading (Language & literacy)—
- Reading in specific content areas

Number & numerical operations (Math)—
- Making exchanges between equivalent sets of coins

MATERIALS

- *Pigs Will Be Pigs* by Amy Axelrod
- Paper
- Pencil
- Money manipulatives

ASSESSMENT

- Observe children as they manipulate the "money." Do they correctly identify the different coins, count out the amounts, and add everything all up?

EXTENSIONS

- Have children use the menu in the book to choose another meal the Pigs could afford.

- Help children plan and hold a bake sale to raise money.

- Have the class save money for a class project, pet, materials or equipment, field trip, or something else special.

MODIFICATIONS

- Have children use calculators to add up the money.

- Have children work in pairs.

MILK MONEY

STORY

Annabelle Swift, Kindergartner by Amy Schwartz

WORKSHOP SUMMARY

Students figure the cost of the class's milk for a day if everyone bought it. This activity is child-directed and can be completed by following the student instructions.

INSTRUCTIONS

You may want to read the story to the whole class a day or so before beginning this workshop.

1. Using the number of students in the classroom and the cost of milk per student, the group finds the cost of the class's milk. There are many ways to do this; encourage students to work together to come up with a method.

2. The group writes down the total they arrive at and explains how they found this total.

ASSESSMENT

- Collect the papers and assess for accuracy. Also look at the way each group solved the problem.

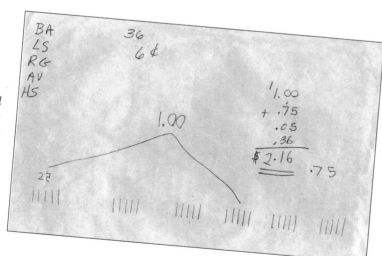

One class divided the number of students into groups of five to make it easier to total the value of their milk money.

KEY EXPERIENCES

Language, symbols, & graphing (Math)—
- Talking about, picturing, and writing about addition and subtraction events
- Writing multi-digit numbers

Number & numerical operations (Math)—
- Grouping and regrouping objects to correspond to the values of digits in multi-digit numbers; making exchanges between equivalent sets of coins

MATERIALS

- *Annabelle Swift, Kindergartner* by Amy Schwartz
- Calculators
- Money manipulatives
- Cost of milk at your school
- Paper
- Pencil

EXTENSIONS

- Have students find the cost of lunches for the class.
- Have students add the cost of snacks to the cost of the lunches.

MODIFICATIONS

- Offer suggestions and support as necessary.

Pasha   25¢

Noelle   25¢

Michael 25¢

Anu   25¢

José   25¢

TEN PENNIES FOR A DIME RESOURCE LIST

Axelrod, Amy. (1997). *Pigs will be pigs.* New York: Aladdin Paperbacks.

Brisson, Pat. (1993). *Benny's pennies.* New York: Bantam Doubleday Dell Publishing Group, Inc.

Burns, Marilyn. (1993). *The $1.00 riddle book.* New York: Addison Wesley Longman. (This book is out of print, but you may be able to obtain a copy from your library.)

Gill, Shelley, and Deborah Tobola. (2000). *The big buck adventure.* Watertown, MA: Charlesbridge Publishing.

Schwartz, Amy. (1991). *Annabelle Swift, kindergartner.* New York: Orchard Books Watts.

Viorst, Judith. (1978). *Alexander, who used to be rich last Sunday.* New York: Atheneum.

Williams, Vera B. (1982). *A chair for my mother.* New York: Mulberry Paperback Books.

HOW BIG?
HOW WIDE?
HOW TALL?

GRADE 2

HOW BIG? HOW WIDE? HOW TALL?
Workshops at a Glance

How High? Students measure the height of their newspapermen with string. *The Fattest, Tallest, Biggest Snowman Ever.*	**String Bodies*** Students design a string body based on the length of their own torso, arms, and legs. *The Fattest, Tallest, Biggest Snowman Ever.*	**The Fattest, Tallest, Biggest Idea** Students plan and build or create something they believe is the tallest, biggest, or fattest. *The Fattest, Tallest, Biggest Snowman Ever.*
How Big Is Your Castle? Each group builds a sand castle at the sand table and measures its height, width, and length. *The Fattest, Tallest, Biggest Snowman Ever.*	**Two Ways to Weigh*** Using a balance scale and a hanging spring scale, students weigh objects in the room. *Me and the Measure of Things.*	**Marking Time With Shadows*** Students mark the passage of time by their shadows. *The Grouchy Ladybug.*
Inching Along Students use inchworm manipulatives to measure things in the story. *Inch by Inch.*	**How Many Feet?** Each student measures the width of the classroom using his or her feet. *How Big Is a Foot?*	**A Book of Sizes*** Each student creates a book of objects in order from smallest to largest. *Is a Blue Whale the Biggest Thing There Is?*

*Requires direct teacher involvement during all or part of the workshop

The workshops in *How Big? How Wide? How Tall?* encourage children to examine and compare things in their world with the aid of standard and nonstandard, familiar and nonfamiliar, measurement tools. Nonstandard tools introduce students to the concept of measuring objects and help them to see the need for using standardized measurements. In these workshops students will examine weight, height, length, width, and time. In some workshops, after students have measured several objects they place them in order based on a particular aspect of their size.

Six books are suggested for use with this set of workshops. The main book used is *The Fattest, Tallest, Biggest Snowman Ever* by Bettina Ling. Jeff, who is never the best at anything and desperately wants to be, builds what he claims is the biggest snowman. Maria believes that perhaps *hers* is the biggest, so the two use a variety of measurement tools to try to find out for sure. In *Me and the Measure of Things* by Joan Sweeney, readers learn how tools such as rulers, scales, cups, and baskets are used to measure things in their everyday world. The book also discusses standard measuring units, including ounces, gallons, pounds, inches, miles, and bushels.

Time is the quantity measured in *The Grouchy Ladybug* by Eric Carle. Grouchy because it cannot have its breakfast to itself, a ladybug goes in search of a creature big enough to pick a fight with. Each hour of the day it meets a larger and more menacing animal, until it arrives back where it started, humbled and just in time for dinner. Another character who meets some not-so-friendly animals is the inchworm in *Inch by Inch* by Leo Lionni. The inchworm is about to be eaten by a robin when he offers to measure the robin's tail. Impressed by the inchworm's talent, the robin takes him to measure some other birds. Trouble looms again for the inchworm when the nightingale threatens to eat him if he cannot measure her song, but luckily the inchworm is tricky as well as talented. Like the inchworm, the talent of the Chief Carpenter's apprentice in *How Big Is a Foot?* (Rolf Myller) gets him into trouble. Asked to make a bed for the queen that is six feet long and three feet wide, the apprentice mistakenly uses his own foot as the measurement instead of the king's foot, which is much larger. Thrown in jail for making the bed too small, the apprentice finally realizes what went wrong and rights his mistake. "Large" is a relative concept, as illustrated in a big way in Robert E. Wells's *Is a Blue Whale the Biggest Thing There Is?* Although the blue whale is the biggest animal on earth, readers learn that it is by no means the Biggest Thing There Is. Progressing from whales to mountains to outer space, the book tries to capture the enormity of our immeasurable universe.

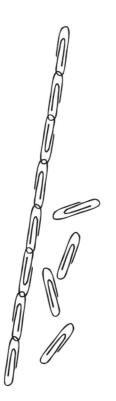

MATERIALS

- *The Fattest, Tallest, Biggest Snowman Ever* by Bettina Ling
- Variety of art materials
- Regular-sized and jumbo paper clips
- Standard and nonstandard measuring tools

HOW BIG? HOW WIDE? HOW TALL?
Whole-Group Introductory Lesson

INSTRUCTIONS

This lesson will require additional time.

Talk with the class about the differences between height, width, and length. Help them define these words by using the classroom and objects they can see as examples.

Ask the class what tools we use to measure things—for instance, rulers, scales, clocks, measuring cups, and so on. (An excellent introduction to measurement is Joan Sweeney's *Me and the Measure of Things*, 2001, New York, Crown Publishers. This book is also used as the basis for one of the workshops in this section.) Discuss also nonstandard measurement tools, such as string, paper clips, unit blocks, and so on. Have them explain how these items can be used to measure objects—for instance, laid end to end, made into a chain, and so on. Have a variety of tools on hand to show the class.

Read *The Fattest, Tallest, Biggest Snowman Ever*. In the story, Jeff and Maria decide to use paper clips to measure their snowmen. They continue to measure their creations using other standard and nonstandard measurement tools. Discuss what they used to measure the snowmen.

Explain that students are going to make and measure "newspapermen" (similar to snowmen but constructed from newspaper). Brainstorm ways to make the newspapermen, such as taping with masking tape, stapling, tying with string, gluing, using clay or playdough for facial features, and so on.

Divide the class into small groups to build and name their newspapermen. Give them as much time as they need. When the newspapermen are completed, explain that the groups will use paper clip chains to measure them, as Jeff and Maria did in the story. Have the class decide whether to use regular or jumbo paper clips, and discuss why all groups need to use the same size (to compare the newspapermen more accurately).

Using the paper clips, each group measures its newspaperman's width (this is an excellent opportunity to teach the word *circumference* if the creations are three dimensional). Groups compare their measurements and list the newspapermen in order from smallest to largest on the board.

Careful planning and working together enabled these students to create a large Pokémon character, which they measured and compared to their classmates' creations, including a snowman.

HOW HIGH?

STORY

The Fattest, Tallest, Biggest Snowman Ever by Bettina Ling

WORKSHOP SUMMARY

Students measure the height of their newspapermen using string. This workshop is child-directed and can be completed by following the student instructions.

INSTRUCTIONS

1. The group uses string to measure the height of each newspaperman created in the whole-group introductory lesson. Each child in the group has a job:

    -   The floor holder holds the string at the floor.

    -   The head holder holds the string at the top of the newspaperman's head.

    -   The cutter cuts the string.

    -   The comparers place the cut strings from all the newspapermen in order from shortest to tallest, making sure they are labeled with the newspapermen's names. The names can be written on a piece of masking tape attached to the string.

    -   The sentence writers write down the newspapermen's names in order of height on the sentence strips, using the words *first, second, third,* and so on.

2. The group compares the strings and the sentences to make sure everything is in the correct order.

Mr. News is first, Word Lady is second . . . .

KEY EXPERIENCES

Language, symbols, & graphing (Math)—
-   Using "first, second, third, ..." to describe position

Measurement of continuous quantity (Math)—
-   Comparing lengths by side-by-side matching

MATERIALS

-   Newspapermen from whole-group introductory lesson, identified with the name given by each group
-   String
-   Masking tape
-   Pen
-   Scissors
-   Blank sentence strips

ASSESSMENT

- Have students display the strings, and assess for accuracy in placing the strings in order from shortest to tallest.

- Check students' sentences for accuracy.

EXTENSIONS

- Have students measure the strings to the nearest inch using rulers.

- Ask students to draw their perfect snowman.

MODIFICATIONS

- None needed.

STRING BODIES

STORY

The Fattest, Tallest, Biggest Snowman Ever

WORKSHOP SUMMARY

Students design a string body based on the length of their own torso, arms, and legs. This workshop is teacher-facilitated.

INSTRUCTIONS (TEACHER-FACILITATED)

This activity may take more than one workshop period to complete.

1. Have each person in the group choose a partner.

2. Using string, students take turns measuring their partner's head from the top to the chin. They cut the string and label with a piece of masking tape. (See Illustration 1.)

Illustration 1

3. Students measure the circumference of their partner's head by putting the string at the top of the head again, then wrapping it under the chin and back around to the top. They cut this string and label. (See Illustration 2.)

4. Each child uses the two lengths of string to outline his or her own head on butcher paper. Children lay the string measuring the length of their head on the paper and lay the other string (the circumference of their head) around it. They use the crayons to draw around the second string and to add details to the face. They can cut it out now, or wait until later.

5. Students measure the length of their partner's neck from under the chin to the top of the collarbone.

Illustration 2

KEY EXPERIENCES

Measurement of continuous quantity (Math)—
- Comparing lengths by side-by-side matching

Measuring, testing, & analyzing (Science)—
- Measuring by producing a length to match another length

MATERIALS
- String
- Scissors
- Butcher paper in a variety of colors
- Crayons
- Tape

6. Students continue by measuring each other's torso from the collarbone to the waist. They also measure from shoulder to shoulder and from hip to hip.

7. They lay the three strings from step 6 on a piece of butcher paper and draw around them to make an upper body for their string person.

8. They measure each other's arms from shoulder to wrist and cut the string. On butcher paper, they outline their hands and cut them out.

9. Children measure their partner's legs from waist to ankle and cut the string.

10. Finally, students stand on a piece of butcher paper and outline their shoes (or feet) and cut out.

11. To assemble:

    The children tape the neck to the back of the head.

    Tape the torso to the base of the neck.

    Tape the arms to the torso.

    Tape the hands to the arms.

    Tape the legs to the base of the torso.

    Tape the shoes or feet to the legs.

12. Have children add details to the bodies, then display.

Measuring parts of the body requires students to use some unusual measurement techniques.

ASSESSMENT

- Take anecdotal notes as children make their measurements and assemble the bodies.

- Note how children follow the directions and work together.

EXTENSIONS

- Have students place the string bodies in order by height.

- Have students measure their arms, legs, and height with a ruler. Compare with one another.

MODIFICATIONS

- Give children directions one step at a time.

- Make a simple diagram showing the different parts to be measured and how to assemble them.

- Use thicker string for children who have trouble grasping the thinner string.

- Demonstrate the instructions ahead of time on a large doll or stuffed bear.

THE FATTEST, TALLEST, BIGGEST IDEA

STORY

The Fattest, Tallest, Biggest Snowman Ever

WORKSHOP SUMMARY

Students plan and build or create something they believe is the tallest, biggest, or fattest. This workshop is child-directed and can be completed by following the student instructions.

INSTRUCTIONS

This activity may take more than one workshop period to complete.

1. Members of the group can choose to work individually or in small groups. They write a plan (in addition, they can draw their plan, if they wish) to build something that is the biggest, tallest, or fattest. The plan should include what they are going to build, what materials they will use, and how they will construct it.

2. Give the groups ample time to build.

KEY EXPERIENCES

Designing, building, fabricating, & modifying structures or materials (Science)—
- Designing and building more complex structures

Writing (Language & literacy)—
- Expressing thoughts in writing

MATERIALS
- Paper
- Pencil
- Variety of open-ended materials (depends on what the groups decide to use and what is available in the classroom)

ASSESSMENT

- Look for creativity and organization of ideas, flexibility in following plan, elaboration, teamwork, and ability to carry out plans.

EXTENSIONS

- Have students choose an appropriate measuring tool(s) and measure their creation.

- Have students draw a diagram of their project.

- Have students write a how-to explaining how to use their product, if applicable.

MODIFICATIONS

- Brainstorm as a group several ideas for what to build, and let children choose from these.

- Give students a limited choice of materials to use, such as construction toys, sand (for example, for building castles), or scrap materials.

- Have children illustrate their plan, list the steps in it, or write a paragraph of the plan, as appropriate.

HOW BIG IS YOUR CASTLE?

STORY

The Fattest, Tallest, Biggest Snowman Ever

WORKSHOP SUMMARY

Each group builds a sand castle at the sand table and measures its height, width, and length. This workshop is child-directed and can be completed by following the student instructions.

INSTRUCTIONS

Before beginning the workshop, discuss with students how they would like to measure the sand castles they will be building. Do they want to use blocks, paper clips, or some other object? They must agree upon a standard, and it must consist of discrete objects that can be counted (or a certain length of string, yarn, or similar material). If your students are not familiar with bar graphs, demonstrate how they will record the information.

1. Students work together at the sand table to build a castle.

2. They photograph their creation and write their group name on the photo.

3. Students measure the length of the sand castle using the chosen standard and record the length on the appropriate graph.

4. Students repeat step 3 for the width and height.

5. As a whole group, compare the height, length, and width of all the castles.

KEY EXPERIENCES

Designing, building, fabricating, & modifying structures or materials (Science)—

- Designing and building simple structures

Language, symbols, & graphing (Math)—

- Making simple bar graphs

MATERIALS

- Sand
- Sand table or tubs or trays for sand
- Water
- Containers, tools, and other materials for building
- Length, Width, and Height graphs, pp. 169–171 (one of each—all groups will record on the same graph)
- One marker of a different color for each group
- Polaroid camera and film

ASSESSMENT

• Compare the graph information with the actual measurements of the sand castles.

• Note how students approach the activity and divide up the tasks.

EXTENSIONS

• Have groups write a story using the sand castle as the setting.

• Ask students to compare and contrast the castle photographs.

MODIFICATIONS

• Divide groups in half if there are too many students to work on one castle together.

• Provide assistance as needed for measuring the castles and documenting the data.

LENGTH

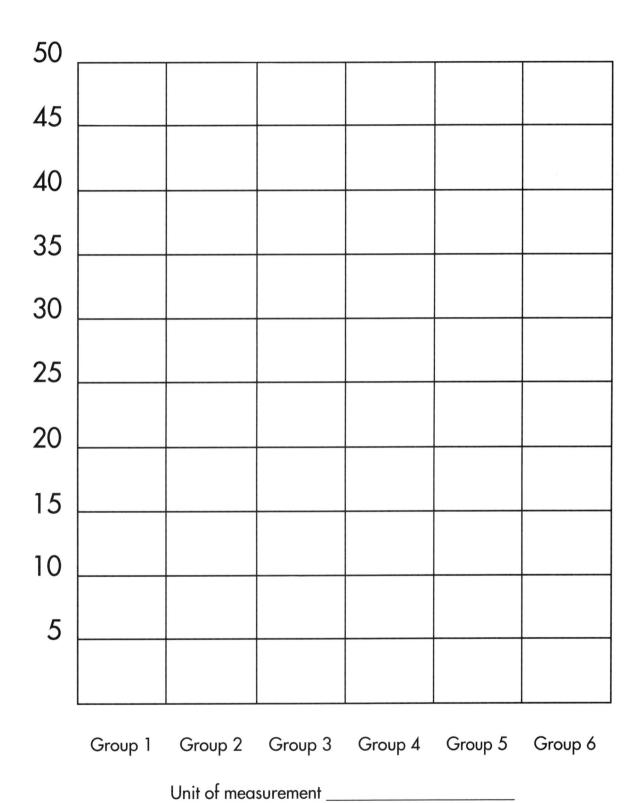

Group 1   Group 2   Group 3   Group 4   Group 5   Group 6

Unit of measurement _____

WIDTH

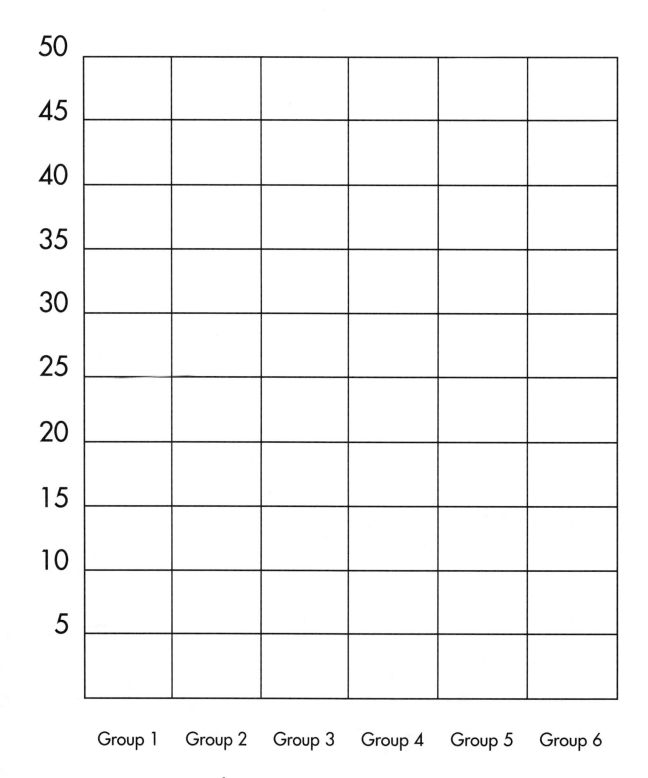

50
45
40
35
30
25
20
15
10
5

Group 1   Group 2   Group 3   Group 4   Group 5   Group 6

Unit of measurement _____

[Handout 2: How Big Is Your Castle?]

This is a reproducible page.

HEIGHT

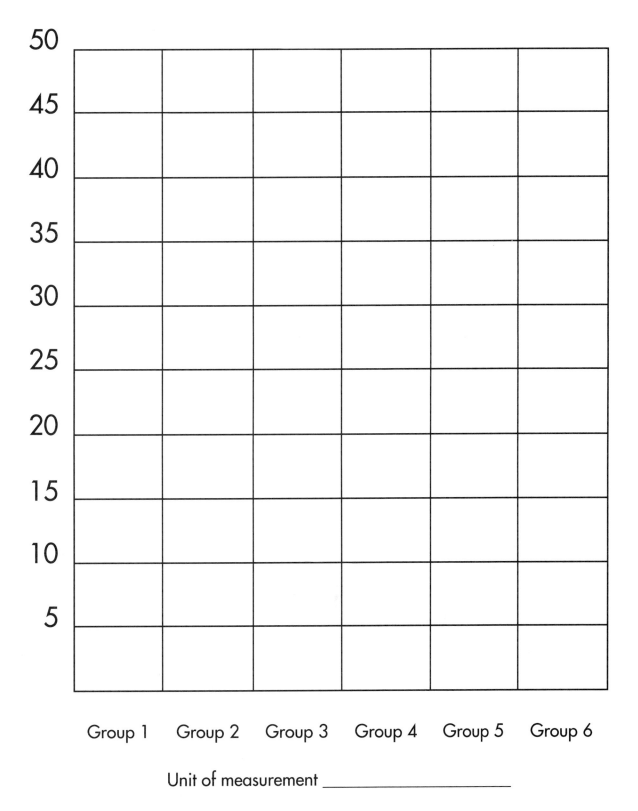

50
45
40
35
30
25
20
15
10
5

Group 1   Group 2   Group 3   Group 4   Group 5   Group 6

Unit of measurement _____

[Handout 3: How Big Is Your Castle?]

TWO WAYS TO WEIGH

STORY

Me and the Measure of Things by Joan Sweeney

WORKSHOP SUMMARY

Using a balance scale and a hanging spring scale, students weigh objects in the room. This workshop is teacher-facilitated.

INSTRUCTIONS (TEACHER-FACILITATED)

1. Ask each member of the group to choose an object or two to weigh on the two scales.

2. Demonstrate and discuss the way a balance scale works. Ask students to predict the order of the objects, from lightest to heaviest.

3. Have students weigh all of the objects on the balance scale and then place them in order by weight. Compare with their predictions.

4. Discuss the way a hanging spring scale works. Again, have them predict the order of the objects.

5. Have students measure the objects on the spring scale, then place them in order. Did the scales give the same or different results? Is one scale more accurate than the other? Ask students to explain why or why not.

6. On the notebook paper, have the group write observations about the activity individually, including a comparison of the order of the objects according to each scale.

KEY EXPERIENCES

Measurement of continuous quantity (Math)—

- Comparing weights by balance
- Comparing weights of objects by the extent they stretch a spring or elastic; ordering objects by weight

Writing (Language & literacy)—

- Writing in specific content areas

MATERIALS

- Balance scale
- Gram weights
- Hanging spring scale
- Variety of objects to weigh
- Paper and pencil

A balance scale (left) and a spring scale (right) provide students with experiences in using nonstandard and standard measurement units.

ASSESSMENT

- Did students understand the differences between the two scales and how each one works? Were they able to use the results from the first measurement to improve their predictions in the second?

- Did students correctly place the objects in order by weight?

- What did students learn from this activity, as evidenced by their written observations?

EXTENSIONS

- Use other types of scales and compare the accuracy of each.

- Ask students how they would weigh larger objects. Examine differences between ounces, pounds, and tons (or grams, kilograms, and metric tons).

MODIFICATIONS

- Designate objects for students to weigh.

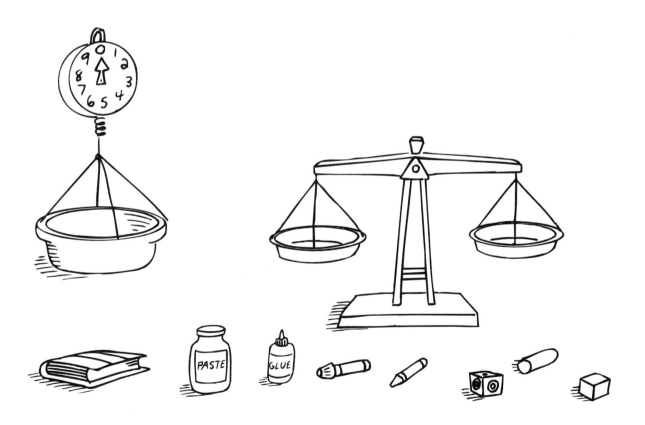

MARKING TIME WITH SHADOWS

KEY EXPERIENCES

Movement, time, & speed (Math)—
- Timing by use of a sand timer
- Using rotational scales (kitchen timer)

Language, symbols, & graphing (Math)—
- Drawing and tracing shapes

Observing, predicting, & controlling change (Science)—
- Observing and identifying a change
- Repeating an activity that produces a change to gain awareness of possible causes

Writing
- Writing in specific content areas

MATERIALS
- *The Grouchy Ladybug* by Eric Carle
- Circular clock
- Chalk
- Sand timer or egg timer
- Paper and pencil
- A sunny day!

STORY

The Grouchy Ladybug by Eric Carle

WORKSHOP SUMMARY

Students mark the passage of time by the movement of their shadows. This workshop is teacher-facilitated.

INSTRUCTIONS (TEACHER-FACILITATED)

1. On a sunny day, gather the group outside on a large concrete or blacktop area. Have each child choose a partner.

2. Have one child stand while the partner outlines his or her feet on the ground with chalk.

3. Have the partner outline the child's shadow and write the time inside the shadow.

4. Have the partners change places and repeat steps 2–3.

5. Set the timer for 10 minutes.

6. While waiting for the timer to go off, read *The Grouchy Ladybug* to the group.

7. When the 10 minutes are up, have the first child in each pair stand in his or her foot outline. Partners repeat steps 3–4.

8. Set the timer for another 10 minutes. Ask the children to predict what will happen to the shadows. For the remainder of the time, children may discuss the story, play on the blacktop, or participate in another activity.

9. Have students repeat steps 3–4.

10. Have students observe the way their shadows have changed. Ask each child to write a summary explaining the activity and what he or she observed. What is happening to make their shadows change position?

ASSESSMENT

- Read children's observations. How do they explain the movement of their shadows?

EXTENSIONS

- Discuss sundials. Make (or have students make) a paper plate model and use a flashlight to demonstrate the movement of the sun over time.

- Look closely at *The Grouchy Ladybug.* Ask students how we would know that time was passing if there were no clock to tell us (by the position of the sun).

MODIFICATIONS

- Let children write the summary with their partner.

INCHING ALONG

STORY

Inch by Inch by Leo Lionni

WORKSHOP SUMMARY

Students use inchworm manipulatives to measure things in the story. This workshop is child-directed and can be completed by following the student instructions.

INSTRUCTIONS

If your students have never used the Inchworms before, let them explore them ahead of time. They are flexible and link together.

1. The group reads *Inch by Inch.*

2. Students go through the story again, using string to measure what the inchworm measured. The items are also listed on the handout.

3. As students measure, they cut the string and tape it under the corresponding name on the list. It should be fully stretched when taped (and looped around if too long to fit in the space provided).

4. Once all string measurements have been made, students use the Inchworm manipulatives to measure the strings.

5. On the line next to the name of each bird, students write the number of Inchworms it took to equal the string for that bird.

KEY EXPERIENCES

Measurement of continuous quantity (Math)—

- Comparing lengths by side-by-side matching
- Measuring to the nearest unit (non-standard)

Measuring, testing, & analyzing (Science)—

- Measuring by producing a length to match another length

MATERIALS

- *Inch by Inch* by Leo Lionni
- Inchworm manipulatives (available through ETA/Cuisenaire elementary math catalog)
- Paper and pencil
- String
- Scissors
- "Measuring Birds" handout, pp. 178–179 (one per group)
- Tape

In this workshop students measure objects not directly but by producing a length to match another length.

ASSESSMENT

- Check for accuracy of string and Inchworm measurements.

- Ask students to explain why they first measured with the string. Do they understand that the string and Inchworms both measure the same thing?

- Note how students go about measuring some of the more difficult items, such as the flamingo's neck.

EXTENSIONS

- Before the workshop, ask students how they could measure the birds in the story. Give them an opportunity to try out their ideas before introducing the string and Inchworms.

- Have students measure a variety of objects in the room with the Inchworm manipulatives.

- Ask students to write the names of the animals in the story in order by length. Which was the shortest and which was the longest? They could also predict the order ahead of time and compare to the actual measurements.

- Ask students to write some suggestions for measuring the nightingale's song.

MODIFICATIONS

- Provide more than one copy of the book if possible.

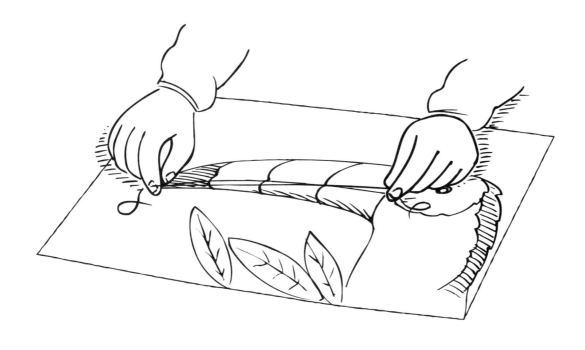

Name _____

MEASURING BIRDS

Robin's tail  _____

Flamingo's neck  _____

Toucan's beak  _____

[Handout 1: Inching Along]

This is a reproducible page.

Name _____

MORE BIRDS

Heron's leg  _____

Pheasant's tail  _____

Hummingbird  _____

HOW MANY FEET?

STORY

How Big Is a Foot? by Rolf Myller

WORKSHOP SUMMARY

Each student measures the width of the classroom using his or her feet. This workshop is child-directed and can be completed by following the student instructions.

INSTRUCTIONS

1. The group reads the story and discusses the problem with the queen's bed. What was wrong with it? How did the apprentice correct the problem? Would the class have the same problem if students measured something using their feet? What do they think would happen if they all measured the width of the classroom with their feet?

2. Each member of the group measures the width of the classroom using his or her feet, heel to toe. Before beginning, each student predicts how many footsteps it will take to measure the width.

3. Each child colors in the space on the graph that indicates the number of feet it took him or her. Students write their name or initials on the line underneath the graph.

4. Students talk about whether their predictions were correct. Who measured the smallest amount? Largest amount? What does this tell students about their feet?

5. Ask them what they could use to get an accurate measurement of the room. How would they know the measurement was correct if they used this tool?

KEY EXPERIENCES

Movement—
*   Moving in locomotor ways

Measurement of continuous quantity (Math)—
*   Comparing length by side-by-side matching
*   Measuring to the nearest unit (nonstandard)

Language, symbols, & graphing (Math)—
*   Making simple bar graphs

MATERIALS

*   *How Big Is a Foot?* by Rolf Myller
*   "How Wide Is Our Room?" graph, p. 182 (one per group)
*   Markers of various colors

In this workshop students learn firsthand the reason standard measurements had to be created!

ASSESSMENT

- Check bar graphs for accuracy.

- Take anecdotal records of the discussions that occur. Note children's understanding of why there are different measurement results when different tools or standards are used.

EXTENSIONS

- Have students measure the width of the room using rulers or meter sticks.

- Have students write a story (similar to *How Big Is a Foot?*) in which difficulties arise because of a lack of standardized measurement. Have them act out the story for the rest of the class.

MODIFICATIONS

- Have a partner help a child keep track of the number of feet as he or she measures.

- Ask children to think of alternative ways for children who are nonmobile to measure the room. For instance, a child in a wheelchair might count how many times he or she spins the wheels while going across the room.

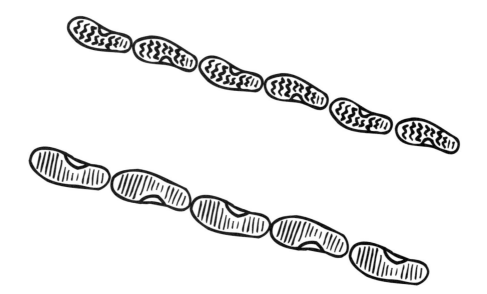

HOW WIDE IS OUR ROOM?

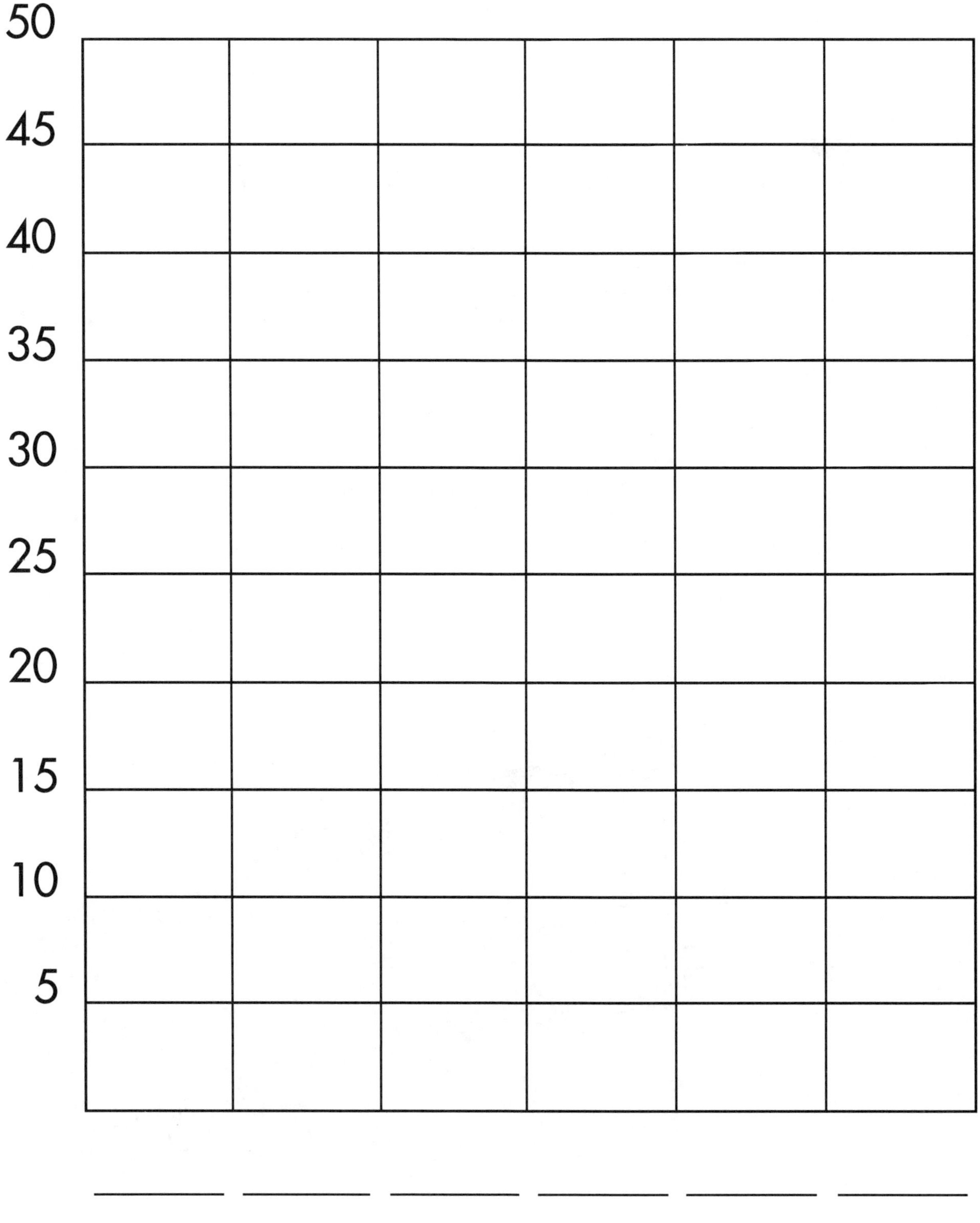
50
45
40
35
30
25
20
15
10
5

[Handout 1: How Many Feet?]

A BOOK OF SIZES

STORY

Is a Blue Whale the Biggest Thing There Is? by Robert E. Wells

WORKSHOP SUMMARY

Each student creates a book of objects in order from smallest to largest. This activity is teacher-facilitated.

INSTRUCTIONS (TEACHER-FACILITATED)

1. Read the story and discuss. What were some of the "smaller" things in the book? Some of the largest? Can students think of very large objects and where they might fit in the order of objects in the book?

2. Have the group think about other categories of objects that are of different sizes—for instance, animals, objects in the classroom, family members, or their toys at home. Ask them to choose a category to make a book about. The group can agree on one category, or each student can choose a different one. Have them make a list of 5–10 objects in their chosen category in order from smallest to largest.

3. Using the list, each student designs a book about his or her objects. The shape of the book, illustrations, and what they write about is up to them. However, the objects must be in order from smallest to largest. This could be shown in the written portion of the book, for example, "My Teenie Beanie is smaller than my regular Beanie Baby."

4. Publish the book and share with the other groups.

ASSESSMENT

- Assess students' understanding of ordering by size.

- Assess students' comparative statements.

KEY EXPERIENCES

Geometry & space (Math)—

- Ordering three or more objects by size; inserting additional objects into an ordered series

Writing (Language & literacy)—

- Expanding the forms of composition: Transactional mode (expository, argumentative, descriptive)

- Publishing selected compositions

MATERIALS

- *Is a Blue Whale the Biggest Thing There Is?* by Robert E. Wells

- Paper and pencils

- Construction paper

- Variety of art materials

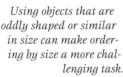
Using objects that are oddly shaped or similar in size can make ordering by size a more challenging task.

EXTENSIONS

- Collect several sets of items of different sizes and place in individual bags. Have students choose a bag and make a new book about the items, or write comparative statements about the size of the items.

- If students have chosen to make a book about their toys at home, ask them afterwards to measure the toys and record their findings.

- Have students brainstorm synonyms for small and large, such as tiny, teeny tiny, itty bitty, gigantic, huge, enormous. Can they think of objects that could be described by each word?

- Have students choose a different criteria by which to order items, such as width, height, volume, and so on.

MODIFICATIONS

- Choose the items students will place in order.

- Encourage students to choose a category of objects they can see as they work on their book, such as items in the classroom, rather than items they can't see, such as toys at home or family members.

HOW BIG? HOW WIDE? HOW TALL? RESOURCE LIST

Carle, Eric. (1977). *The grouchy ladybug.* New York: Scholastic, Inc.

Ling, Bettina. (1997). *The fattest, tallest, biggest snowman ever.* New York: Scholastic, Inc.

Lionni, Leo. (1960). *Inch by inch.* New York: Scholastic, Inc.

Myller, Rolf. (1962). *How big is a foot?* New York: Dell Publishing.

Sweeney, Joan. (2001). *Me and the measure of things.* New York: Crown Publishers.

Wells, Robert E. (1993). *Is a blue whale the biggest thing there is?* Morton Grove, IL: Albert Whitman & Co.

STUDENT
INSTRUCTION
CARDS

FOOD COLLAGE

1. Pick a shape and a piece of paper.
2. Glue your shape on the top of your paper.
3. Cut out foods that match your shape.
4. Glue the pictures on the paper.

SHAPE SCULPTURE

1. Bend the pipe cleaners into a circle, square, triangle, and rectangle.
2. Make one more shape.
3. Put all the shapes together to make a sculpture. Twist a small pipe cleaner where the shapes join.

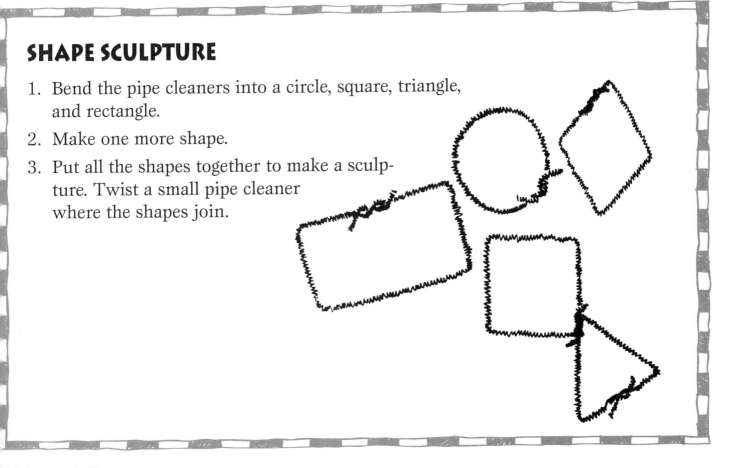

This is a reproducible page.

SHAPE HUNT

1. Look through the book. Name all the shapes you see on each page.

2. Take a chart and a pencil. Look for things in the room that are a ▭ , ▢ , ◯ , and △ .

3. Draw the things you see where they go on the chart. Draw at least one thing for each shape.

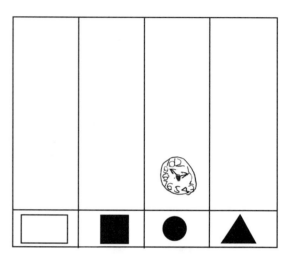

PATTERN BLOCK PICTURES

1. Make a design with the blocks.

2. Make the same design with the paper shapes on the construction paper.

3. Glue the paper shapes.

I SPY SHAPES

1. Choose a shape from the shape list.

2. Write the shape word in the blank at the top of your page.

    Example: I spy a <u>rectangle</u>.

3. Draw your shape in black crayon on the page.

4. Draw a picture. Make your shape part of the picture.

5. What did you make your shape into? Write it in the blank at the bottom of the page.

    Example: It is a <u>door</u>.

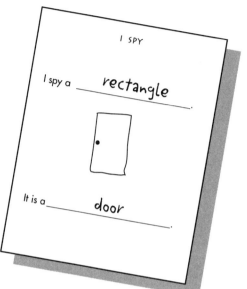

COMPUTER SHAPES

1. With a partner, look at the shapes activity on *Millie's Math House*.

2. Make a picture with the shapes. You can follow a pattern or make up your own.

3. Print your picture and color it.

4. Write about your picture, or have your teacher write for you.

This is a reproducible page.

JUMP-ROPE CHANTS

1. Pick a jump-rope chant.

2. One person jumps rope. The rest say the chant.

3. After the chant, count the number of jumps.

4. On the paper, write the number of jumps.

5. Everyone takes a turn jumping. Write down the number of jumps for everyone.

6. Line up by the number of jumps everyone made.

7. Show your teacher how you lined up.

HOW MANY DOTS?

1. Guess how many dots are on the dot paper.

2. Write your guess on the back.

3. Count the dots. Write the number under the dots.

4. Did you guess more? Did you guess less? Who guessed closest?

5. Look at the jar. Guess how many things are in it.

6. Write your guess on the piece of paper.

7. Take the objects out. Count them.

8. Who guessed the closest?

This is a reproducible page

HOW MANY SECTIONS?

1. Pick a fruit. Put it on the plate.

2. Write the name of your fruit on your handout.

3. Guess how many sections your fruit has. Write the number on the "How Many Sections?" chart.

4. Break your fruit into sections. Count how many. Did you guess right?

5. Write the number of sections on your handout and on the chart.

6. Find a crayon the same color as your fruit. On the handout, draw how many sections your fruit has.

HOW MANY SECTIONS? (CONT.)

2

7. Which fruit has the most sections? Which one has the least?

8. Put all the handouts together. Start with the one that has the fewest sections and end with the one that has the most.

9. Eat the fruit!

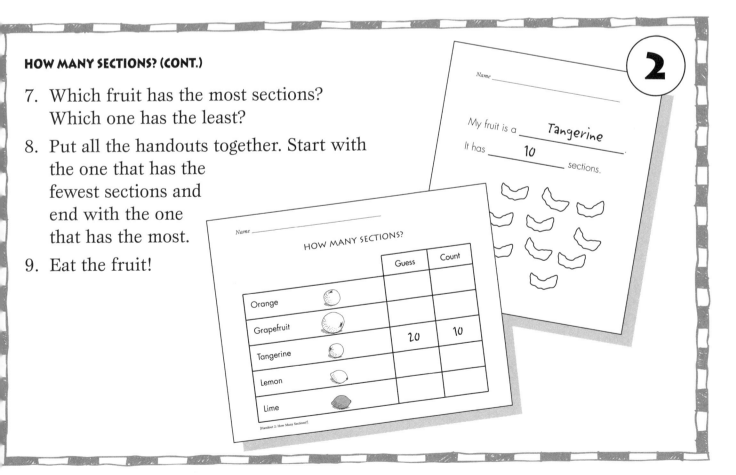

Name _____

My fruit is a _____ Tangerine _____

It has _____ 10 _____ sections.

Name _____

HOW MANY SECTIONS?

		Guess	Count
Orange			
Grapefruit		20	10
Tangerine			
Lemon			
Lime			

[Handout 2: How Many Sections?]

This is a reproducible page.

COUNTING ON CRITTERS

1. Look at the bug book to get ideas for your bug.

2. Glue three or four circles to make a body. Glue one circle for the head.

3. Pick things to draw or glue on your bug. Make a different number of each thing.

4. Name your bug.

BEGINNING, MIDDLE, AND END

1. Form two groups.

2. One group works on the computers with *Sammy's Science House.*

3. The other group puts the picture cards in order by what happened in the story.

4. On the long piece of paper, draw your favorite part of the story. Make sure it has a beginning, a middle, and an end.

5. Switch groups.

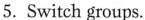

JUMP NARROW, JUMP WIDE

1. Stand in line at the jump rope that is taped down.

2. Put the second jump rope on the first tape mark. Take turns trying to jump over this rope.

3. Move the second jump rope to the second line. Start at the first jump rope again, and try to jump over the next rope.

4. Keep moving the jump rope to the next line. Jump until you cannot reach the next line.

5. Mark the line you jumped to with a piece of tape. Put your name on the tape.

6. Measure how far you jumped. Use string, paper clips, or blocks.

Miranda jumped 6 blocks.

WHICH IS TALLEST? WHICH IS SHORTEST?

1. Build a tower of blocks.

2. On paper, write the names of the builders. First, write the name of the person with the shortest tower, then the name of the person with the next tallest tower. Keep going in order until you write the name of the person with the tallest tower.

3. On the Block Tower Graph, color in one square for each block in your tower. **OR,** glue one square paper on the graph for each block in your tower.

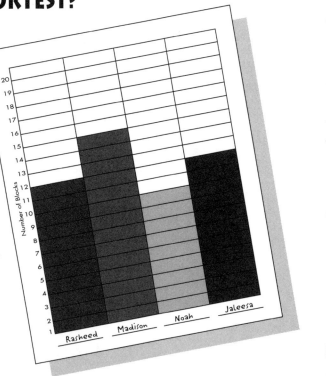

This is a reproducible page.

WHAT'S LIGHTEST, WHAT'S HEAVIEST?

1. Everyone finds two objects that will fit on the scale.

2. Look at the objects. On the handout, write the objects in the order you think they go, from lightest to heaviest. Do not feel them yet.

3. Take turns putting one object on the scale. Put cubes on the other side until the scale is even.

4. Count the number of cubes used for each object.

5. Write the number on the handout next to the name of each object.

6. Did you guess the right order of the objects? Write the objects in the right order on the handout.

GREAT BIG BEARS, LITTLE TINY BEARS

1. Put the bears in order from littlest to biggest.

2. Now look at the bears' feet. Put the bears in order from the littlest feet to the biggest feet.

3. Pick another way to put the bears in order.

4. Write a sentence that tells about the order of the bears or the size. Use words like *between, next to, before, after, smaller, biggest.*

   Examples: Carter's bear comes after Maria's bear.
   Keisha's bear is the biggest.

Keisha's bear is the biggest.

WAYS TO GET TO 12

1. Make two groups from your 12 counters.

   Example: 4 bears and 8 bears

2. On the handout, write the two numbers that add up to 12.

   Example: 4 + 8 = 12

3. Make as many different groups as you can. Write the numbers that add up to 12 on the handout.

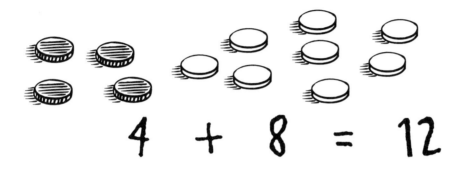

$$4 + 8 = 12$$

PICTURING ADDITION

1. Look at the pictures in the book.

2. Choose a different idea to draw, like food, animals, or sports.

   Example: 4 blueberries and 6 strawberries

3. Write the number sentence that will match your picture.

   Example: 4 + 6 = 10

4. Draw your picture.

5. Write a word problem about your picture.

   *Example: 4 blueberries and 6 strawberries
   equal 10 berries*

$$4 \text{ blueberries} + 6 \text{ strawberries} = 10 \text{ berries}$$

HOW MANY LETTERS?

1. Count the number of letters in each word on the Word List.

2. Write the words where they go on the chart.

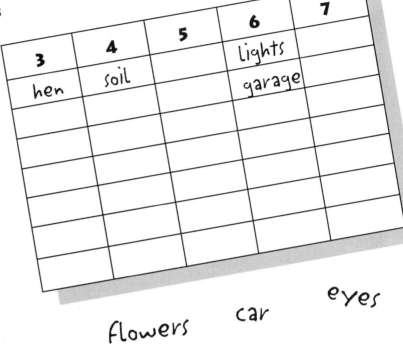

3	4	5	6	7
hen	soil		lights	
			garage	

flowers   car   eyes

DRAW TWO

1. Draw two number cards from the bag.

2. Make a train with two colors of cubes. Use the same number of cubes as on the cards.

3. Draw the same train on the grid paper. Color in one section for each cube.

4. Write the number sentence that tells about your train.

5. Pick two new cards and do it again.

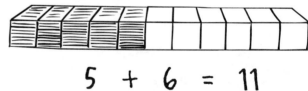

5 + 6 = 11

ODD OR EVEN?

1. Find a partner.
2. On the handout, next to 11, write *odd*.
3. Pick another number on your paper. Take that many counters and put them into two groups.
4. If there is one left over, write *odd* next to that number on your paper. If there are no counters left over, write *even* next to that number.
5. Do this for all the numbers.
6. Answer the bonus question.

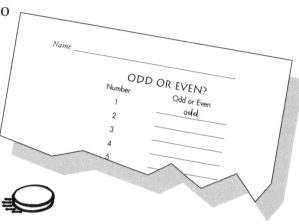

Number	Odd or Even
1	
2	odd
3	
4	
5	

$1.00 WORDS

1. Write the first spelling word *down the side* of your paper.
2. Next to each letter, write how much money it is worth. Use the Alphabet List to find out.
3. Add up the amounts of all the letters. Use a calculator if your teacher says to.
4. Write the total and compare your answer with the rest of the group's.
5. If someone's answer does not match the rest of the group's, work together to make it right.

M	.13
O	.15
N	.14
E	.05
Y	.25
	.72

DRAW A PENNY

1. Read *Benny's Pennies.*

2. Without looking at a penny, draw a picture of the head and tail. Set the timer for two minutes.

3. Look at the penny under the magnifying glass. Set the timer for one minute.

4. Go back to your drawing and add anything you forgot. Don't look at the penny!

5. Compare the penny to your drawing again. Add anything else you missed.

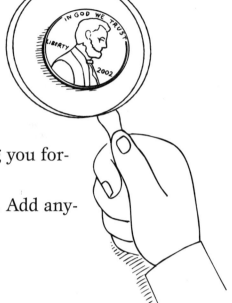

HOW MUCH WATER CAN A PENNY HOLD?

1. Put the penny on the paper towel. Get down so your eyes are right next to the penny.

2. Slowly, one drop at a time, add water to the penny. Count each drop.

3. Write down the number of drops the penny holds before the water spills over.

4. Dry the penny and try again. See if you can get more drops on the penny.

5. Write down the highest number of drops.

This is a reproducible pag

PENNY ART

1. Pick a piece of paper.

2. Trace several pennies on your paper to make a design or picture. **OR,** trace and cut out several pennies and glue them on another paper to make a design.

3. Use materials in the art area to finish your picture.

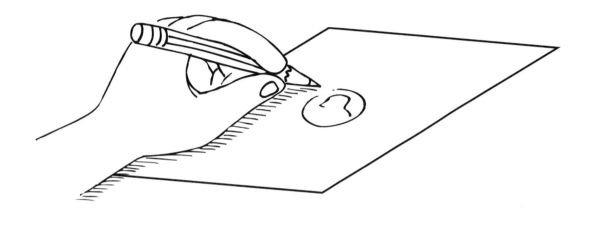

MILK MONEY

1. Figure out how much milk would cost if everyone in the class bought one carton. Use the number of students in the class and the cost of one carton.

2. Write down your answer. Explain how you got it.

This is a reproducible page.

HOW HIGH?

1. Measure how tall each newspaperman is by using string. Give everyone a job:

   The **floor holder** holds the string at the floor.

   The **head holder** holds the string at the top of the newspaperman's head.

   The **cutter** cuts the string.

   The **comparers** put the cut strings from all the newspapermen in order from shortest to tallest. Write the name of each newspaperman on a piece of masking tape and tape it to the string.

   The **writers** write the newspapermen's names in order on the sentence strips. Use the words *first, second, third,* and so on.

2. Compare the strings and the sentences to make sure everything is in the right order.

   Mr. News is first, Word Lady is second . . . .

THE FATTEST, TALLEST, BIGGEST IDEA

1. Decide if you want to work alone or with someone else.
2. What can you build that would be the biggest, tallest, or fattest? It should be something you can make with things in the room.
3. Write your plan. Tell what you are going to build, what you will use to build it, and how you will make it.
4. Build what you have planned.

We will build the tallest building...

HOW BIG IS YOUR CASTLE?

1. Build a sand castle with your group.
2. Take a picture of it. Write your names on the picture with a marker.
3. How long is the sand castle? Measure.
4. Mark how long it is on the "Length" graph.
5. How tall is the castle? Measure.
6. Mark how tall it is on the "Height" graph.
7. How wide is the castle? Measure.
8. Mark how wide it is on the "Width" graph.

INCHING ALONG

1. Read *Inch by Inch.*
2. Use pieces of string to measure the animals in the book. Measure what the inchworm measured.
3. Cut the string. On the handout, tape each string under the bird that it goes with.
4. Measure the strings with the Inchworms.
5. In the blank next to each bird, write the number of Inchworms.

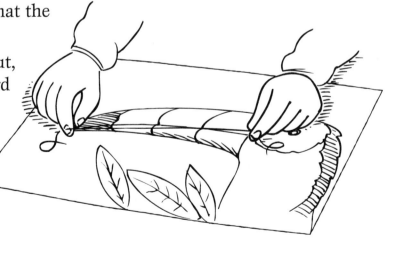

This is a reproducible page.

HOW MANY FEET?

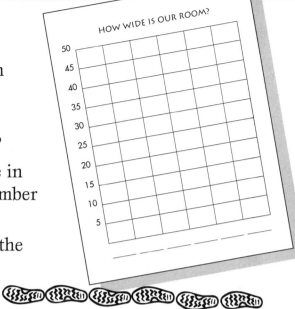

HOW WIDE IS OUR ROOM?

1. Read the story. Talk about the problem with the bed.

2. How many of your feet do you think it will take to measure how wide the classroom is?

3. Walk across the room, putting your feet one in front of the other, heel to toe. Count the number of steps.

4. Color in the space on the graph that shows the number of feet you counted. Write your name on the line under the space you colored in.

5. Did you guess the right number of feet? Who had the most? Who had the least?

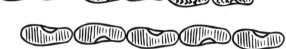

This is a reproducible pag

INDEX

ABOUT THE AUTHORS

Kathy Morrison holds a doctorate in early childhood education and is an assistant professor in that field at the University of Texas at Tyler. Her areas of expertise include science and technology for young children, family communication, and the constructivist approach to education. Kathy has been a preschool and elementary consultant for High/Scope Educational Research Foundation since 1991. She has conducted training on technology for young children, family communication, and language-based workshops at the annual International High/Scope Conference. Kathy is the author of the previous book in this series, *Literature-Based Workshops for Language Arts* (with Tina Dittrich and Jill Claridge), as well as of *Family Friendly Communications* (National Association for the Education of Young Children), and *Beginning Science: The Essential Elements* (T. S. Denison).

Tina Dittrich has worked for Grapevine/Colleyville Independent School District in Grapevine, Texas, for eight years. She taught third and fifth grade, spent two years as a specialist in gifted and talented services, and is currently back in the classroom teaching fifth grade. Tina has conducted training sessions on elementary math and gifted education at various conferences, including the High/Scope International Conference and the Texas Association for the Gifted and Talented (TAGT).

Jill Claridge is an educational diagnostician and consultant in private practice in Bedford, Texas. She provides educational testing for children and adults with learning differences and conducts workshops for teachers and administrators in public and private schools. She also mentors teachers working with young children. Previously, Jill worked for 25 years as a teacher, school principal, and diagnostician at Child Study Center in Fort Worth, Texas. She was also an adjunct professor in special education at Texas Christian University in Fort Worth. Jill holds a doctorate in special education and is a field consultant for High/Scope in the preschool and elementary areas.

Workshop-Related High/Scope® Resources

To order the children's books that accompany the workshops in this book, please contact High/Scope: Phone: 1-800-40-PRESS Fax: 1-800-442-4FAX

ITEM#	TITLE	List Price	H/S Retail
BK-EHB776	Alexander, Who Used to Be Rich Last Sunday	$16.00	**$13.60**
BK-EPB420	Anabelle Swift, Kindergartner	$6.95	**$5.91**
BK-EHB500	Anno's Counting Book	$16.95	**$14.41**
BK-EPB346	Benny's Pennies	$6.99	**$5.94**
BK-PHB115	Big Fat Hen	$16.00	**$13.60**
BK-EHB494	A Chair for My Mother	$15.95	**$13.56**
BK-EHB380	Each Orange Had 8 Slices	$15.95	**$13.56**
BK-EPB394	The Fattest, Tallest, Biggest Snowman Ever	$3.99	**$3.39**
BK-EHB762	Goldilocks and the Three Bears	$16.99	**$14.44**
BK-EHB390	The Greedy Triangle	$15.95	**$13.56**
BK-EHB775	The Grouchy Ladybug	$16.95	**$14.41**
BK-EPB382	How Big Is a Foot?	$3.99	**$3.39**
BK-EPB334	How Many Teeth?	$4.95	**$4.21**
BK-EHB369	The Icky Bug Counting Book	$16.95	**$14.41**
BK-EPB479	Inch by Inch	$5.95	**$5.06**
BK-EHB355	Is a Blue Whale the Biggest Thing There Is?	$13.95	**$11.86**
BK-EHB844	Me and the Measure of Things	$12.95	**$11.01**
BK-EHB431	Pigs Will Be Pigs	$15.00	**$12.75**
BK-EHB436	Round Is a Mooncake: A Book About Shapes	$13.95	**$11.86**
BK-EHB381	Shapes, Shapes, Shapes	$15.95	**$13.56**
BK-EHB117	Ten Black Dots	$16.00	**$13.60**
BK-EPB109	12 Ways to Get to 11	$6.99	**$5.94**
BK-PHB163	The Very Hungry Caterpillar	$19.99	**$16.99**

*All books subject to publisher's availability

To see a full listing of High/Scope® products, visit our Web site: www.highscope.org

Related High/Scope® Resources

Elementary Curriculum Guides

Foundations in Elementary Education: Overview

This guide and accompanying video can help you get acquainted with the High/Scope® approach to elementary education. They provide an effective summary to use in explaining the High/Scope® approach to parents, teachers, and administrators. Guide may be purchased separately.

Guide: BK-E3007 $10.95;
Guide and video: BK-E3011SET $15.95

C. Hohmann. Soft cover, 56 pages, 1996.
1-57379-005-2 (manual & video); 0-929816-94-3 (manual).

Foundations in Elementary Education: Movement

For classroom teachers, physical education and music specialists, teachers working with special populations, and parents. Part 1 describes the program's philosophy, goals, and strategies. Part 2 contains information on nine movement key experiences and 80 related activities incorporating active learning. This curriculum guide complements the elementary music guide.

BK-E3006 $39.95

P. Weikart and E. Carlton. Illustrated, soft cover, 418 pages, 1995.
0-929816-93-5.

Foundations in Elementary Education: Music

Part 1 provides a general framework for implementing music in the elementary classroom. Part 2 contains information related to 21 music key experiences and associated activities.

BK-E3005 $39.95

E. Carlton and P. Weikart. Illustrated, soft cover, 375 pages, 1994. 0-929816-60-9.

Foundations in Elementary Education: Music Recordings

Sing these 30 delightful songs based on important musical concepts as you enable students to develop their musical foundation. Each song is sung with simple accompaniment, so you can quickly join in. This music is designed to accompany the book *Foundations in Elementary Education: Music* by Elizabeth B. Carlton and Phyllis S. Weikart.

Cassette: BK-E3101-C $10.95; CD: BK-E3201 $15.95

Coproduced by Elizabeth B. Carlton and Phyllis S. Weikart. 1995. Cassette 1-57379-000-1 or CD 1-57379-001-X.

Learning Environment

This lavishly illustrated, comprehensive guide offers essential information on the physical setting, daily schedule, and teacher-child interaction strategies for active learning classrooms. Describes how to arrange and equip the learning environment and set up a daily schedule to support a balanced range of individual, small-group, and large-group learning experiences.

BK-E3004 $24.95

C. Hohmann and W. Buckleitner. Illustrated field test ed., soft cover, 156 pages, 1992. 0-929816-39-0.

Language & Literacy

In High/Scope® classrooms, the balanced reading perspective in which phonic, semantic, and syntactic cues are integrated provides the fundamentals of literacy in developmentally appropriate ways. Children use oral and written language in a dynamic learning environment. High/Scope's key experiences in speaking and listening, writing, and reading are presented, together with many enjoyable classroom-tested activities. Packed with useful information and essential teaching strategies.

BK-E3001 $24.95

J. Maehr. Illustrated field test ed., soft cover, 256 pages, 1991. 0-929816-23-4.

Mathematics

Discusses how math relates to children's stages of thinking and the adult's role. Contains over 100 hands-on activities designed for small-group learning. High/Scope's math key experiences are also presented.

BK-E3002 $24.95

C. Hohmann. Illustrated field test ed., soft cover, 304 pages, 1991. 0-929816-24-2.

Science

Help children discover science through firsthand experiences. Guided by six groups of science key experiences, teachers learn to recognize the aspects of scientific thinking and problem solving that are developing in children. The 54 activities described can be conducted with inexpensive or found materials.

BK-E3003 $24.95

F. Blackwell and C. Hohmann. Ilustrated field test ed., soft cover, 216 pages, 1991. 0-929816-25-0.

To order these or any other High/Scope® products, contact High/Scope® Press: phone (800)40-PRESS fax (800)442-4FAX

To see a full listing of High/Scope® products, visit our Web site: www.highscope.org

Related High/Scope® Resources

Program Evaluation

Elementary Program Implementation Profile (PIP): Administration Manual

An ideal evaluation tool for all elementary grade settings. This manual helps you rate your program site according to physical environment, daily schedule, adult-child interaction, instructional methods, staff development, and home-school collaboration. The elementary PIP can also be used for training and pinpointing specific areas needing improvement. The manual is separate from the assessment forms.

BK-E3015 $6.95

Soft cover, 8 pages, 1997. 0-57379-031-1.

Elementary PIP Assessment Pak

PIP Assessment Forms in sets of 25.

BK-E3016SET $24.95

1-57379-032-X.

Elementary Science Activity Series

Each activity book presents a variety of interesting science activities, along with standard information designed to help teachers determine each activity's appropriateness for their students, plan its implementation, and help children focus on a range of related learning experiences.

1. Life and Environment
BK-E3008 $22.95

Soft cover, 216 pages, illustrated, 1996.
1-57379-009-5.

2. Structure and Form
BK-E3009 $22.95

Soft cover, 184 pages, illustrated, 1996.
1-57379-010-9.

3. Energy and Change
BK-E3010 $22.95

Soft cover, 176 pages, illustrated, 1996.
1-57379-011-7.

Elementary Curriculum Videotapes

Special Elementary Video Package
BK-E3013SET $104

Set of four color videos, 65 min. 1-57379-059-1.

Active Learning

Empower children to become independent problem solvers, critical thinkers, and creative participants in a rapidly changing world.

BK-E2003 rental $10; purchase $30.95

Color video, 17 min., 1991. 0-929816-27-7.

Classroom Environment

Learn why the daily schedule includes time for High/Scope's plan-do-review process and small-group instructional workshops. Video shows how High/Scope® classrooms accommodate children's physical growth, increase their intellectual growth, and foster social and emotional development.

BK-E2004 rental $10; purchase $30.95

Color video, 17 min., 1991. 0-929816-28-5.

Language & Literacy

Speaking and listening, writing and reading are integrated experiences in High/Scope® elementary classrooms. Learn why the school's role is to provide opportunities for children to build on and extend their emerging language skills. This balanced approach addresses the fundamentals of literacy.

BK-E2001 rental $10; purchase $30.95

Color video, 17 min., 1990. 0-929816-21-8.

Mathematics

See the High/Scope® mathematics curriculum in action in actual elementary classrooms across the U.S.! This video presents an overview of High/Scope's developmentally appropriate and effective method of mathematics instruction. See how enjoyable and stimulating small-group and individual activities in mathematics can be organized and presented.

BK-E2002 rental $10; purchase $30.95

Color video, 14 min., 1990. 0-929816-22-6.

To order these or any other High/Scope® products, contact High/Scope® Press: phone (800)40-PRESS fax (800)442-4FAX
To see a full listing of High/Scope® products, visit our Web site: www.highscope.org